COLLINS GEM
CATS
a mine of information

GW00669948

COLLINS GEM
HORSES
& PONIES
a mine of information

a mine of information

COLLINS
QUEENS
a mine of information

a mine of information

COLLINS GEM
SNAKES
a mine of information

COLLINS GEM
SPIDERS
a mine of information

COLLINS GEM
STRESS
Survival Guide
a mine of information

COLLINS· GEM
TAROT
a mine of information

COLLINS GEM
WINE
Guide
a mine of information

COLLINS GEM
WORLD
atlas
a mine of information

COLLINS GEM
YOGA
a mine of information

COLLINS GEM
ZODIAC
Types
a mine of information

Marie Farquharson is a journalist who contributes to leading national newspapers and magazines and has written widely on topics ranging from family health to women's issues.

HarperCollins Publishers
Westerhill Rd, Bishopbriggs, Glasgow G64 2QT

Created and produced by
Grapevine Publishing Services, London

First published 2001
Reprint 10 9 8 7 6 5 4 3 2 1 0

Illustrations by David Mostyn
Photography by Christina Jansen
Photo on page 49 courtesy of The Bowen Technique

ISBN 000 710149–X

Printed in Italy by Amadeus S.p.A.

Contents

Introduction

There was a time when complementary medicine was dismissed as quackery or a fad that would never last. Despite such predictions, however, interest in complementary therapies has boomed alongside people's growing concern for a healthy lifestyle. At a time when the boundaries of medical science are being tested and barriers are pushed in areas such as gene therapy and laser surgery, many people are becoming increasingly distrustful of conventional medicine. Disenchantment with medical science, which many regard as synthetic, detached, and, in some cases, dangerous, has led to people turning in droves towards a more natural approach to healthcare. Studies suggest that between one third and half of all adults in Europe have used some form of complementary therapy at some time, the most popular being osteopathy, chiropractic, homeopathy, aromatherapy, and acupuncture, according to a Consumers' Association Survey.

The popularity of complementary medicine has obliged the medical profession to sit up and take non-conventional therapies more seriously, so that their use alongside mainstream medicine is now booming. More than 40 per cent of GPs offer complementary medicine within their NHS practices and more than 70 per cent regularly refer their patients to its practitioners. And more doctors than ever are training in complementary therapies so that they can offer their patients the best of both mainstream and complementary medicine.

WHAT IS COMPLEMENTARY MEDICINE?

The most significant difference between conventional and complementary medicine lies in their approach to the definition and treatment of disease. Whereas conventional medicine is diagnosis-led, complementary practitioners aim to treat the whole person. In practice this means that conventional doctors will look at your symptoms. For complementary practitioners, illness is seen as a disturbance in physical and mental wellbeing and treatment is given to stimulate the body's natural self-healing abilities.

The complementary practitioner's approach to treatment is known as a holistic one, the key principle being that any treatment must be planned around the person as a whole (holism comes from the Greek word meaning whole). So in addition to any physical symptoms a practitioner will also take into account your emotional, mental and spiritual health.

Holistic practitioners believe that your mind and body have a natural tendency to keep themselves in a state of balance or homeostasis. When this balance is disrupted, ill health is often the result. The therapist's job is to work with you to galvanise your body's self-regulating abilities.

HOW TO CHOOSE A THERAPY

Because complementary treatment aims to trigger your body's natural self-healing abilities, in theory any therapy can help with any problem, but it is important to choose a therapy with which you feel comfortable. If you hate people touching your feet, for example, then reflexology is probably not for you. The following questions are designed to make you think about your attitudes to health and should help you to home in on the approaches that might suit you best.

From the following list, choose the five factors that you consider are most important to your health. Each one is marked either (a) or (b). When you have finished, count up the number of (a) answers and the number of (b) answers you have chosen and check your score.

- A natural well-balanced diet (a)
- Time and space to relax (b)
- Regular exercise (a)
- Healing energy flowing through you (b)
- Plenty of fresh air (a)
- Managing stress (b)
- Getting rid of toxins (a)
- Spirituality (b)
- A well-functioning body structure (a)
- Family (b)
- No money worries (a)
- Friends (b)

ANALYSING YOUR SCORE

Mostly a's: the condition of your body and environment is important to you; as such you may be more comfortable with body-oriented therapies such as aromatherapy, yoga and osteopathy.

Mostly b's: emotional and spiritual harmony play a key role in your ideas of good health; as such you may find that therapies such as Chinese herbalism and Ayurveda suit you best.

This section will help you to examine how responsible you are for your health. Choose the five statements you agree with most strongly and count your score as above.

- My health depends on how much care I take of myself. (**a**)

- No matter what I do, if a bug is going around I'll catch it. (**b**)

- If I regularly visit a practitioner I can prevent illness. (**a**)

- My health is vulnerable to accidental events. (**b**)

- I have the ability to heal myself. (**a**)

- I can only stay well by getting professional treatment. (**b**)

- My health is my responsibility. (**a**)

- My health is the responsibility of others. (**b**)

- By taking care of myself I can stay healthy. (**a**)

- When I get ill I have to let it run its course so that nature has time to do its healing work. (**b**)

- I fall ill when I don't look after myself properly. (**a**)

ANALYSING YOUR SCORE

Mostly a's: you assume considerable responsibility for your health. This means that you may prefer a therapy in which you can be actively involved such as relaxation, acupressure, and t'ai chi.

Mostly b's: you prefer to put yourself in the hands of professionals and let them look after you. Practitioner-led therapies such as Western herbalism and homeopathy may therefore suit your temperament best.

In this section you'll examine the personal preferences that may influence your choice of therapy. Choose the five statements you agree with most strongly, then count the number of a's, b's and c's.

- I like to be massaged or touched. (**a**)

- I find it easy to take pills. (**b**)

- I find it easy to talk about my emotions. (**c**)

- I don't worry about getting undressed in front of a practitioner. (**a**)

- I am happy to make dramatic changes to my diet. **(b)**

- I'm drawn to the theory of using my mind to improve my health. **(c)**

- I don't mind needles. **(a)**

- I like taking remedies and potions. **(b)**

- I find it easy to share experiences in a group situation. **(c)**

- I enjoy the experience of having my body worked on. **(a)**

- I like the sensation of my body working well. **(b)**

- I prefer to talk privately about my feelings. **(c)**

ANALYSING YOUR SCORE

Mostly a's: you will probably be at ease with hands-on therapies such as Alexander Technique and shiatsu.

Mostly b's: you may well respond best to therapies based on diet, medicines or remedies such as nutritional therapy and Bach flower remedies.

Mostly c's: you seem to be open to exploring your emotions. Check out therapies that work on the mind and emotions such as psychotherapy, counselling, and colour therapy.

You should now have a better idea of the kind of therapies that could suit your temperament. It's also worth considering other factors that could affect your choice:

- If you need the reassurance of clinical trials backing up a therapy's efficacy you may be better off choosing one of the better-researched disciplines such as acupuncture, meditation and Alexander Technique.

- Personal recommendations may help your choice.

- It's always a good idea to let your doctor know that you intend to embark on a complementary therapy, and if you value her opinion it's a good time to sound her out about what she thinks.

- Is there a therapy that has a brilliant track record of dealing with your particular problem?

Always check that your therapist is professionally qualified, and if you have a bad feeling about a consultation, trust your judgment. Always be as informed as you can and be wary of anyone claiming 'miracle' results.

HOW TO CHOOSE A THERAPIST

So how do you find a reputable, professionally qualified therapist who you can trust? While many therapies are strongly regulated, others are not, which means that there may not be a watertight way of knowing whether your practitioner is adequately skilled. All this means that finding a good practitioner can be a matter of trial and error. If you have someone in mind, ask to speak to her clients, or ask for recommendations. If you are considering chiropractic, acupuncture or osteopathy, ask your doctor if she can recommend a therapist.

QUALIFICATIONS/CREDENTIALS

- Always check that your practitioner is professionally qualified. What was her training? Where did she train? And for how long?

- Check out her experience. How many years has she been practising? And if she is relatively inexperienced, is she working under a supervisor?

- Is your practitioner happy to tell your doctor about any treatment you receive?

PROFESSIONAL ORGANISATIONS AND ASSOCIATIONS

- Is the practitioner a member of a recognised association and is the register open to the public?

- Does the organisation have a code of professional practice?

- Is there a complaints system or disciplinary procedure?

- Is the practitioner happy to give the address and phone number of the organisation with which she is registered?

RELATIONSHIP WITH YOUR PRACTITIONER

Having a practitioner you trust and feel comfortable with is vital. Always be wary of anyone guaranteeing a cure, and don't agree to any changes in your medication without consulting your doctor first. In most cases your first appointment will begin with the practitioner asking you a host of questions about your health and lifestyle. Use this time to quiz her in return. When the session is over ask yourself:

• How were your questions dealt with? Were they answered clearly and thoroughly?

• Did the therapist conduct herself professionally?

FINANCE

Consider the following questions before embarking on a course of treatment:

• How much does the treatment cost? Can you get it by referral, which could bring down the cost?

• Can you claim for the treatment on your private health insurance?

• How long will you need treatment?

• Does the practitioner have professional insurance that would allow you to claim compensation in the case of negligence?

Now turn to the A–Z section for a description of each therapy and contact details for organisations that can help you find a good therapist.

A–Z OF COMPLEMENTARY THERAPIES

Acupuncture

Acupuncture has been practised in China for more than 3,500 years and is part of a wider system of healthcare called Traditional Chinese Medicine (TCM).

Central to TCM are the concepts of yin and yang, opposing but complementary forces whose balance within the body is essential for health, and *chi*, the vital energy or life-force which drives every cell of the body and protects the body from disease. *Chi* flows around the body through 12 meridians or channels, six of which are yin and six of which are yang. Dotted along these meridians are 365 acupuncture points.

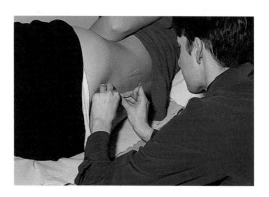

Acupuncturists believe that a harmonious flow of *chi* is essential to health. Any disruption upsets the balance of yin and yang, leading to illness. To restore balance, the acupuncturist stimulates the relevant meridians either by the insertion of fine needles into the specific points or by applying pressure to the acupuncture points (*tsubos*) with a fingertip or thumb (acupressure). In the West the use of acupressure has largely been overshadowed by SHIATSU.

● CONDITIONS TREATED

It can be used to treat most problems, but it is commonly used for aches and pains ranging from arthritis to back pain, sports injuries, and migraine, as well as asthma, digestive disorders, depression and anxiety, hay fever, nausea, high blood pressure and women's health.

● WHO CAN'T BE TREATED?

Just about anyone can be treated, even animals, but tell your practitioner if you are pregnant, as certain acupuncture points should not be stimulated in pregnancy.

Choosing a practitioner
Contact the British Acupuncture Council,
63 Jeddo Road, London W12 9HQ
Tel. 020 8735 0400 www.acupuncture.org.uk

● **WHAT HAPPENS AT A CONSULTATION**

Your first visit will involve a session of detailed
questions lasting about 45 minutes which enables
the practitioner to assess your condition. The
therapist will also complete the picture of the state
of your health by taking your pulse on both wrists
and examining your tongue (its shape, colour and
coating will give clues as to your overall health).
Depending on your condition, CHINESE HERBALISM
may be recommended as an additional,
supplementary treatment option.

Alexander Technique

The Alexander Technique
was developed in the late
nineteenth century by
Australian actor
Frederick Matthias
Alexander when he began
to lose his voice for no
apparent reason. When,
despite medical treatment, his
condition worsened he set
about finding the answer
himself.

Realising that the problem
occurred during performances

only, Alexander analysed what he did differently when speaking on stage. He found that the relationship between his head and neck and how they related to the rest of his body was crucial: his posture during performance represented a pattern of misuse that affected his voice, which in turn created a general pattern of tension in his body. Gradually he taught himself to override bodily tensions by adopting a natural, stress-free posture.

Alexander Technique is not a therapy as such but a method of re-education which teaches you how to use your body more efficiently, moving with poise and grace. It works on the principle that emotional and physical strain are linked and can become fixed in the muscles, distorting posture and movement. Over time this can cause health problems, such as back pain.

● CONDITIONS TREATED

Alexander Technique teachers don't claim to cure anything, but by helping you to improve the way in which you use your body, they can help to alleviate back pain and musculo-skeletal problems, stress, anxiety, depression, headaches, gastrointestinal disorders, repetitive strain injuries, and postural pain in pregnancy.

● WHO CAN'T BE TREATED?

Anyone can learn Alexander Technique if it is taught by a qualified teacher.

● WHAT HAPPENS AT A CONSULTATION

Alexander Technique is usually taught on a one-to-one basis. Lessons last around 30-45 minutes and a course generally comprises between 25 and 40 sessions. At the start of the first lesson your teacher will ask you what you hope to get from the course. If you have a particular problem ask the teacher if she thinks that Alexander Technique can help and how many lessons you'll need.

You should wear loose, comfortable clothes. The teacher will talk you through everything she does, adjusting your posture and teaching you how to replace bad habits with good ones so that you gain an awareness of how optimum body posture feels and how to achieve it.

At the end of each lesson the teacher may give you some exercises to practise at home.

Choosing a practitioner
To find a qualified Alexander teacher contact
The Society of Teachers of Alexander Technique,
129 Camden Mews, London NW1 9AH
Tel. 020 7284 3338

Applied kinesiology

Kinesiology (pronounced *kin-easy-ology*) means the study of movement of the human body. It was developed as a therapy in 1964 when American chiropractor Dr George J. Goodheart found that he could tell more about a person's health by testing their muscles than by any other method of diagnosis.

Some applied kinesiology methods have long been used by conventional doctors and physiotherapists to test range of movement, but AK practitioners use muscle tests to analyse the cause of illness rather than diagnose and name a specific disease. The practitioner works to find out about the health of the whole person, to pinpoint any imbalances in the body and decide what it needs to correct them. As with ACUPUNCTURE, practitioners believe that imbalances and blockages in

energy flow translate into symptoms, physical or emotional. Kinesiology can prevent illness by rectifying imbalances before they become symptoms.

● CONDITIONS TREATED

Kinesiology is not a cure as such; practitioners aim to find and correct niggling, minor problems that cannot be diagnosed, because they are only the precursors to disease. Food sensitivities, digestive problems, stiff joints, aches and pains and even phobias can be eased.

● WHO CAN'T BE TREATED?

It can help people of all ages and levels of fitness, including babies and pregnant women.

● WHAT HAPPENS AT A CONSULTATION

The first session usually lasts about an hour. It will start with detailed questions about your health and lifestyle. You may then be asked to lie down either clothed or undressed to your underwear, while the practitioner carries out muscle tests. The tests are painless and very straightforward. Typically a practitioner will hold your arm in a particular position to isolate a specific muscle. She will then touch a precise point on your body and press down firmly on your arm while asking you to resist the pressure. If you are able to resist, then that part of the body is healthy. If you can't, it's a sign of an energy imbalance. When your problem has been diagnosed, the therapist may treat you herself (many AK practitioners are trained in some other areas such as massage, osteopathy, chiropractic, nutritional therapy, acupuncture, colonic hydrotherapy and Bach flower remedies), or alternatively, she will recommend a course of treatment elsewhere.

Choosing a practitioner
Contact the Association of Systematic Kinesiology, 39 Browns Road, Surbiton, Surrey
Tel. 020 8399 3215

Aromatherapy

The origins of aromatherapy go back thousands of years. The ancient Egyptians used aromatic plants in cosmetics and for embalming the dead. Hippocrates, the father of modern medicine, recommended aromatherapy baths and scented massage. In England, essential oils were used to ward off the plague. But it was in the 1930s that aromatherapy as we know it today was developed by French chemist René-Maurice Gattefossé. His work was further developed first by French Army surgeon Dr Jean Valnet, who used essential oils as antiseptics in World War II, and later by Madame Marguerite Maury who transformed aromatherapy into a holistic system of care, in which the oils used are chosen according to the individual rather than the symptoms. She was also the first to combine essential oils with massage.

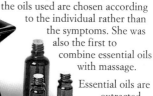

Essential oils are extracted from the flowers, seeds, leaves, bark or roots of plants with medicinal properties. Every plant has its own healing property, though nearly all are anti-fungal and antibacterial. Some are also anti-viral. The smell of essential oils has a direct effect on the limbic system, the part of the brain that governs emotions, and because essential oil molecules are so small they can be absorbed through the skin, and enter the bloodstream and nervous system, thus influencing emotional and physical wellbeing.

● CONDITIONS TREATED

Stress-related conditions such as insomnia and headaches, as well as eczema, acne, digestive problems, asthma, colds, aches and pains, premenstrual syndrome, menopausal complaints, pregnancy, labour and postnatal depression.

● WHO CAN'T BE TREATED?

Aromatherapy can be used to treat most people, including young children. If you are pregnant, have a medical condition such as eczema, high blood . pressure or epilepsy, be sure to tell your therapist who will tailor your treatment accordingly.

● WHAT HAPPENS AT A CONSULTATION

You'll be asked about your lifestyle and medical history. This enables the practitioner to work out which oils are most suited to your needs. From this selection you may be asked to choose your preferred aromas. As most therapists apply the oils in a full-body massage, the treatment room will have a massage table, the lighting is usually soft and relaxing music may be playing in the background. The room should be warm, comfortable and clean. For the massage you will be asked to undress and lie on the massage table with a towel over you. While you do so the therapist will turn away or may leave the room to give you some privacy. During the massage the therapist will talk very little if at all. At the end of the session you may be given oils to use in the bath at home or to put a few drops on a handkerchief and inhale.

Choosing a practitioner
Contact the Aromatherapy
Organisations Council,
PO Box 19834,
London SE25 6WF
Tel. 020 8251 7912.

Art therapy

In the 1940s artists working in psychiatric hospitals noticed that art was a valuable therapeutic tool. They found that patients who were encouraged to paint, draw, work with clay or any other art materials were able to express and free up emotions buried deep in their subconscious.

In art therapy everything has significance. For example, whether you choose to work with pencils or oils will send out a message about the kind of person you are and the kind of problems you have. The therapist will discuss the content of your work with you as well as your approach to it and your feelings about it.

- ## CONDITIONS TREATED

  Psychological and emotional problems, learning disorders, dementia, schizophrenia. Art therapy is useful for people with impaired hearing or speech.

- ## WHO CAN'T BE TREATED?

  A qualified therapist can treat people of all ages with all types of psychological problems.

- ## WHAT HAPPENS AT A CONSULTATION

  Before the first proper appointment the therapist will arrange to meet you for an assessment. You'll be asked about your emotional problems, relationships and lifestyle. The therapist will also want to know what you expect from the therapy and will encourage you to ask any questions you may have. The sessions can be on a one-to-one basis or in a group of about eight people. Each lasts from an hour to an hour and a half. Children's sessions last half an hour. Everything that takes place in the session is confidential. Time is usually allowed within the session for discussion.

Choosing a practitioner Contact the British Association of Art Therapists, Mary Ward House, 5 Tavistock Place, London WC1 9SN
Tel. 020 7383 3774
Send an A4-size sae for their practitioner list.

Autogenic training

Autogenic training is a therapy based on deep relaxation, in which simple mental exercises are used to relieve the effects of stress on your body. It was developed in the 1920s by Dr Johannes Schultz, a German psychiatrist and neurologist. He noticed that when people are hypnotised they enter a deeply relaxed state in which the psychosomatic disorders that affect their daily life are completely absent. Schultz believed that it was possible to bring about these sensations simply by auto-suggestion. Hence he coined the term 'autogenic', meaning generated from within. This term also highlights the essential difference between autogenic training and hypnosis. In the latter, suggestions are planted in your subconscious mind by the therapist. With autogenic training you yourself plant the suggestions to switch on the relaxation response.

● **CONDITIONS TREATED**

Irritable bowel syndrome, asthma, stress-related conditions such as tension headaches, high blood pressure and anxiety, insomnia, premenstrual syndrome, arthritis and colitis.

● **WHO CAN'T BE TREATED?**

People with personality disorders or acute psychoses. Also it's advisable to tell your doctor if you plan to use autogenic training as some medical conditions, such as diabetes, can be affected by it, in which case your medication may need to be adjusted.

● **WHAT HAPPENS AT A CONSULTATION**

Before your first session you'll be asked to attend an assessment and complete a health questionnaire. The training itself may be given in small groups or individually. Lessons are generally an hour long and are taught weekly, usually for about eight weeks. The exercises are all mental ones but are fairly simple to learn. However, they must be practised

Choosing a practitioner
Contact the British Association for Autogenic Training and Therapy, c/o The Royal Homeopathic Hospital, Great Ormond Street, London WC1N 3HR. Send an A4-size sae for their practitioner list.

three times a day every day for a maximum of 15 minutes. About six weeks after your last lesson, you'll have a follow-up appointment to review your progress.

Automated Computerised Treatment System (ACTS)

See RADIONICS

Ayurveda

Ayurveda is the traditional medicine system of India and Sri Lanka. Practitioners believe that everything in the universe is made up of a vital energy, which they call *prana* (known in Traditional Chinese Medicine as *chi*). This energy controls every aspect of your life: when it is in balance it contributes to good health, but when there is an imbalance the result is ill health.

One of the key principles of ayurveda is that of the five elements – ether, air, fire, water and earth – which are forever changing and interacting. These elements can be further classified into three vital energies or doshas – vatha, pitha and kapha – which make up your constitution. Each dosha type has different characteristics. Typically one or two doshas will dominate, so that you will be classed as either a vatha, pitha or kapha type or a combination (vatha/pitha and so on).

Practitioners believe that each and every one of us has a unique constitution and that a strong one is your best defence against illness. During the consultation, you will be advised on your lifestyle, diet and exercise. Ayurveda teaches that the best foods for you are the ones that suit your constitution or doshic type and help to balance excesses in one or other of the doshas.

● CONDITIONS TREATED

Irritable bowel syndrome, constipation, indigestion, eczema, water retention, and circulation problems.

● WHO CAN'T BE TREATED?

Pregnant women or very frail patients can't have the panchakarma treatments, and certain conditions such as cancer and some hernias should not be treated ayurvedically.

• WHAT HAPPENS AT A CONSULTATION

The aim of the first appointment is to enable the therapist to build a detailed picture of you, work out your dominant dosha, and determine where any imbalances lie. To this end you'll be asked a host of questions about your lifestyle, your likes and dislikes, your diet and appetite, your bowel movements and digestive system, your general health and your parents' health. The therapist will also be assessing your shape, size, speech, posture and the way you move. She will also check your eyes, tongue, lips, and even the lines on your face. Finally she will take your pulse from three specific points on each wrist. Once a diagnosis has been made your treatment can begin.

Ayurvedic treatment typically starts by first detoxifying the body to eliminate disease or any blockages or imbalances in the body. This is called panchakarma and involves two or three of the following treatments:

nirhua – oil enema therapy
anuvasana vati – herbal enema therapy
vireka – herbal laxative therapy
vamana – therapeutic vomiting
(this is rarely used today)
vasya – herbal inhalation therapy

Once your system has been cleansed the practitioner may prescribe herbal or mineral remedies to correct and restore balance to your doshas. She will also offer advice on your lifestyle, diet, and exercise. According to ayurvedic medicine the best foods for you are those that suit your constitution.

Choosing a practitioner
Contact the Ayurvedic Medical Association UK, 7 Park Crescent, London W1N 3HE
Tel. 020 8682 3876

See also FASTING

Bach flower remedies

See FLOWER REMEDIES

Bates method

The Bates method is a system of natural vision improvement. It was pioneered by Dr William H. Bates, an American ophthalmologist (1860-1931) who corrected his failing eyesight using his own revolutionary exercises. Bates reasoned that because vision is an unconscious learning process that starts from birth, it can be disturbed by bad habits and any physical, mental or emotional imbalances. Eyesight is not fixed, he claimed, and as well as getting worse it can also get better. The Bates method works by removing any obstacles that are interfering with the normal functioning of the eye.

Practitioners believe that most problems with vision can be traced to two faults: either the eye muscles are too tense or the eye and brain are not co-ordinating as they should be. The skill of the practitioner is to teach people to learn to use their eyes properly.

While many people are able to give up wearing glasses or contact lenses using this system, for some it is not possible to achieve perfect sight. The Bates method can, however, help you to achieve the optimum vision for your own given situation and prevent your eyesight from deteriorating any further.

- ## CONDITIONS TREATED

  Long- or short-sightedness, astigmatism, squints and even glaucoma.

- ## WHO CAN'T BE TREATED?

  The Bates method can be used to help children and adults.

- ## WHAT HAPPENS AT A CONSULTATION

  It normally takes six to ten lessons to learn the basic techniques of the Bates method. Teachers believe that good vision depends on the eyes working together in a relaxed way. They use a series of exercises tailored to your individual needs to relieve strain and improve eye/brain co-ordination. The exercises range from simple blinking movements to juggling, which encourages the eyes to follow the movements of the balls.

Choosing a practitioner
Contact The Bates Association of Great Britain, PO Box 25, Shoreham-by-Sea, BN43 6ZF
Tel. 01273 422090

Biochemic tissue salts

Also known as Schüssler Salts, biochemic tissue salts were developed in the 1870s by Dr Wilhelm Schüssler, a German homeopathic doctor. He believed that many diseases were caused by a lack of one or more of 12 essential minerals, and to correct the deficiency he prescribed minute doses of the relevant mineral/s in the form of homeopathically prepared remedies that he called tissue salts.

● CONDITIONS TREATED

Colds, catarrh, coughs, sore throats, hay fever, headaches, anxiety, indigestion, heartburn, cramp, neuralgia, muscle pain, minor skin complaints.

● WHO CAN'T BE TREATED?

The active ingredients in tissue salts are present in such tiny amounts that they are harmless and so can be used by everyone. Always check with your doctor, however, if you are taking them as a self-help remedy, because your symptoms could be a sign of a more serious problem.

● WHAT HAPPENS AT A CONSULTATION

Tissue salts are commonly prescribed by homeopaths as part of a nutritional programme, but naturopaths and herbalists use them too. So the nature of your consultation will depend on the kind

of practitioner you're seeing. The remedies are
prescribed in the form of small tablets which should
be dissolved under the tongue.

Choosing a practitioner
For tissue salts and professional advice about how
to use them, contact Ainsworth's Homeopathic
Pharmacy, 36 New Cavendish St,
London W1M 7LH
Tel. 020 7935 5330
They are also available in all homeopathic
pharmacies and good health food shops. For
practitioners who use tissue salts, see HOMEOPATHY.

Biodynamic therapy

Biodynamic therapy was developed in the 1960s by
Norwegian psychologist and physiotherapist Gerda
Boyesen. In the course of her work she observed that
many of her clients' stomachs would gurgle loudly,
particularly when releasing emotions, and that massage
could cause patients to be sick. But in both situations
these patients made quicker recoveries than those who
had no physical release. She believed this to be
because emotional and psychological problems register

in the muscles and body organs – particularly the intestines.

Following on from her belief that energy travels through your body as a liquid flowing force (the term 'biodynamic' is her word for this energy), Boyesen argued that this flow can become blocked by emotional and physical factors such as severe shock or injury. When this happens the muscles of the intestines won't work correctly, which undermines the health of your system both mentally and physically in the long term.

● CONDITIONS TREATED

Stress-related illness, such as migraine and lower back pain, as well as angina, MS, Parkinson's disease and rheumatoid arthritis.

● WHO CAN'T BE TREATED?

Biodynamic therapy is not suitable for people in the advanced stages of disease. It's taken up mainly by adults who have problems to work out, but children with psychological problems can also benefit.

● WHAT HAPPENS AT A CONSULTATION

A session usually lasts about an hour. The first one starts with a detailed discussion about your medical history and lifestyle. Because intestinal health underpins biodynamic therapy, the therapist may listen to your intestines with a stethoscope. There is no set course of treatment – the therapist will plan an approach according to your needs. Therapists use a variety of massage techniques to release emotions stored in muscles and encourage energy flow. Treatment is fairly intense and it may unlock old memories or trigger emotional outbursts which you'll be encouraged to express.

Choosing a practitioner
Contact the Gerda Boyesen Centre,
15 The Ridgeway, Acton, London W3 8LW
Tel. 020 8993 5777
www.bodydynamicpsychotherapy.com

Bioenergetics

Bioenergetics is a body-oriented form of
psychotherapy. It was developed in the 1960s by an
American doctor called Alexander Lowen who was a
student of Wilhelm Reich. Like his mentor, Lowen
believed that the body, mind and emotions are closely
linked. Drawing on the work of Reich and Freud,
Lowen created a number of exercises based on those
in t'ai chi and Pilates, designed to release physical
tension and pent-up emotions.

• CONDITIONS TREATED

Stress-related conditions such as irritable bowel
syndrome, ulcers, migraine, asthma, fatigue,
chronic pain, and some mental health problems.

● WHO CAN'T BE TREATED?

Those who are prone to anxiety, who suffer from post traumatic stress disorder or have a history of mental illness such as manic depression or schizophrenia should not try bioenergetics.

● WHAT HAPPENS AT A CONSULTATION

Before your treatment begins you'll have a one-to-one assessment. Practitioners believe that how you deal with stresses and traumas is programmed in your muscles and that your posture provides clues to your mental attitudes and psychological problems. Following this she may advise individual therapy sessions or suggest joining a group or a mix of individual and group therapy.

Group workshops are usually made up of 12 to 20 people. The class may start with general warm-up movements. Exercises focus on areas of tension to unlock repressed memories so that past traumas can be explored. Practitioners will also teach you grounding exercises, as they believe that if you have a good contact with the ground, you will be more in touch with your body and emotions.

Choosing a practitioner
Contact the Chiron Centre, 26 Eaton Rise, London W5 2ER
Tel. 020 8997 5219

Biofeedback

Biofeedback machines were developed in the early 1930s to detect tiny physical responses in the body. At first researchers focused on reading electrical signals from the brain, but in the 1960s American scientists started using biofeedback to train people to control their heart rate and other unconscious functions. Research has shown that using it to relax the shoulder muscles, for example, could ease tension headaches. Biofeedback is usually practised in hospitals and universities but portable devices are available for home use.

● CONDITIONS TREATED

Stress, anxiety, insomnia, headaches, migraine, high blood pressure, irritable bowel syndrome, asthma, incontinence, Raynaud's disease.

● WHO CAN'T BE TREATED?

It can be used by most people in consultation with a qualified practitioner, but advise them if you take any medication.

● WHAT HAPPENS AT A CONSULTATION

The practitioner will ask about your lifestyle, diet and medical history. Once this assessment is complete you will be linked up to the biofeedback machine using a system of electrodes or probes.

There are several different types of machine including some that measure skin temperature or brainwave activity. All work in the same way, sending out signals such as bleeps and flashing lights to 'feed back' information about the changes in your body, and you will be taught how to respond to these signals. You will also be taught breathing exercises to help bring about the desired response. A minimum of six half-hour sessions may be required.

Choosing a practitioner
Biofeedback is increasingly used by GPs so the chances are your doctor may be able to treat you himself. If not, ask him to refer you to a practitioner who uses biofeedback.

Bioresonance therapy

Bioresonance therapy (BRT) was developed in
Germany in the 1970s by a Dr Morell. He believed
that different cells in the body oscillate at different
frequencies – some healthy ('harmonic'), others
unhealthy ('disharmonic'). Using a bioresonance
machine, therapists are able to pick up the body's
oscillations, separate the healthy from the unhealthy,
and then reflect them back to the patient. This
reinforces the body's healthy electromagnetic
frequency and activates its self-healing powers.

● CONDITIONS TREATED

It can be used to treat most conditions but is
particularly effective in the treatment of allergies.

● WHO CAN'T BE TREATED?

BRT can be used to treat people of all ages and
levels of fitness.

Choosing a practitioner
Most bioresonance practitioners in the UK are
medical doctors, vets, surgeons, acupuncturists,
nutritional therapists, osteopaths, chiropractors
and reflexologists using the system alongside their
individual skills. To find a qualified practitioner
using bioresonance call 01938 556800.

● WHAT HAPPENS AT A CONSULTATION

At your first appointment the practitioner will want to assess your general health. He will ask about your diet, lifestyle and medical history. After the assessment treatment will begin. You'll be asked to take off your shoes and socks, then sit on a chair with your feet on two metal plates.

You will then be given two metal bars or balls to hold, each of which is connected to a piece of equipment called a bioresonance machine. The practitioner will programme the machine and let it run its course. Treatment is not painful although some people do experience a tightness and a squeezing sensation.

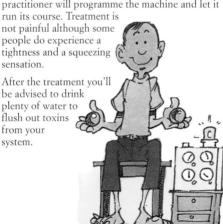

After the treatment you'll be advised to drink plenty of water to flush out toxins from your system.

Biorhythms

Biorhythms are a daily internal cycle that govern physical, emotional and intellectual functioning. They were first charted in Berlin around 1900 by a Dr Wilhelm Fleiss who believed that a male 'solar' cycle (regulating physical health) and female 'lunar' cycle (regulating the emotions) co-exist in everyone. These cycles, he concluded, are the reason why on some days you wake up feeling bright-eyed, clear-headed and on top of the world and other days, for no obvious reason, you feel irritable, tired and unable to concentrate.

Your biorhythms fall into three cycles: the physical cycle is 23 days long and regulates strength, immunity, stamina, sex drive and co-ordination; the emotional cycle is 28 days long and influences mood and creativity; the intellectual cycle is 33 days long and governs memory and concentration.

Peaks in these cycle are said to be times of increased rationality, whereas troughs are marked by increased intuition. As the length of each cycle varies, the peaks and troughs of each rarely occur at the same time, but when they do you are said to be particularly vulnerable.

> **Choosing a practitioner**
> This is a self-help technique. To plot your own biorhythms, get *The Biorhythm Kit* by Jacinthat Crawley (Connections) or check out the website: www.facade.com

● CONDITIONS TREATED

Biorhythm charts are less a treatment than a tool to help you pinpoint the times of the year or month when you'll be at your best and worst physically and emotionally, so that you can plan for holidays, operations, business ventures or projects and know when not to take risks.

● WHO CAN'T BE TREATED?

Biorhythms are basically a self-help technique and charts can be drawn up for people of all ages and levels of fitness.

● WHAT HAPPENS AT A CONSULTATION

To chart your own biorhythms, buy a kit with a calculator, wheel and illustrated instruction book. There are also computer programs available.

Body psychotherapy

See BIOENERGETICS

Bowen Technique

Bowen Technique is a gentle, non-invasive form of bodywork that works on the connective tissue of your muscles. It was originated by Australian healer and industrial chemist Tom Bowen. With no formal training he developed a system of precise and highly specific moves which he combined with home remedies. Bowen only allowed one person to study his work, and it was this man, Oswald Rentsch, who began to train therapists after Bowen's death in 1982.

● CONDITIONS TREATED

Sports injuries, lower back injuries, tension headaches, RSI (repetitive strain injury), respiratory problems such as asthma, and bedwetting.

Choosing a practitioner
Contact European College of Bowen Studies,
38 Portway, Frome, Somerset BA11 1QU
Tel. 01373 461873
www.thebowentechnique.com

● WHO CAN'T BE TREATED

There is one move that should not be used during pregnancy, otherwise it is suitable for anyone from newborns to the elderly and incapacitated.

● WHAT HAPPENS AT A CONSULTATION

A Bowen treatment is around 30-45 minutes long and is performed through light clothing. Practitioners use a series of gentle moves on the muscle and connective tissue along the whole body using the thumb and fingers, which encourages the body to restore itself to good health. The touch is firm but not painful, and helps the body to make its own adjustments to rebalance, relieve tension and reduce pain. Practitioners simply perform the moves and then leave your body to deal with them.

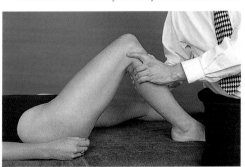

Bowen is very simple but is said to be highly effective, with 80-90 per cent of people only needing one or two sessions. For those who have been in pain for six months or more, however, further sessions may be required.

Breathing and relaxation

In the East breathing and relaxation techniques have been used for centuries to relax the mind and body. Here in the West we're finally recognising their importance as stress management tools.

● CONDITIONS TREATED

Anxiety, depression, high blood pressure, menstrual and menopausal problems, insomnia, fatigue, phobias, panic attacks, asthma, eczema, pain relief, irritable bowel syndrome.

● WHO CAN'T BE TREATED?

Provided they are taught correctly, breathing and relaxation techniques are suitable for all, even small children.

● **WHAT HAPPENS AT A CONSULTATION**

On your initial visit you will be asked about your lifestyle, medical history and any factors or events that may be causing stress. You will be taught a number of relaxation techniques, such as progressive muscle relaxation which involves systematically tensing and releasing all of the main muscle groups in your body.

One of the first exercises you'll learn is abdominal breathing. This is a gentle and relaxing technique that teaches you how to fill and empty your lungs with the minimum of effort.

Loose and comfortable clothing is recommended, and depending on the method being taught you may be asked to sit in a chair or to lie or sit on a mat on the floor.

The initial session consultation will last up to an hour and subsequent sessions will be shorter.

Choosing a practitioner
Many practitioners, especially yoga teachers and therapists and hypnotherapists, teach breathing and relaxation techniques. For relaxation tapes, information about courses and books, contact: The Stress Management Institute, Foxhills, 30 Victoria Avenue, Shanklin, Isle of Wight, PO37 6LS Tel. 01983 868166 www.smtl.org

Buteyko

Buteyko was developed by Russian medical scientist Professor Konstantin Buteyko in the 1950s. He believed that to be healthy you need to breathe properly. In the course of his 40 years of research he found that only one in ten people breathes correctly, and he linked around 200 diseases with poor breathing. According to Buteyko, normal breathing results in a very specific ratio of oxygen to carbon dioxide. If you breathe too deeply or 'overbreathe' you actually deprive your body of essential carbon dioxide, which paradoxically means you get less oxygen; this causes wheezing, tightness and coughing. Hidden hyperventilation often goes unnoticed; asthmatics often overbreathe three or more times. After making this discovery, Professor Buteyko developed

a breathing technique
that enables normalised
breathing and hence the
correct levels of carbon
dioxide.

> **Choosing a practitioner**
> Contact Woodlands
> Health & Allergy Clinic,
> 70 Winchester Road,
> Blaby, Leicestershire
> LE8 4HJ
> Tel. 0116 2772051

● CONDITIONS TREATED

It is primarily used
for asthma but it can help any problem associated
with poor breathing such as heart problems,
emphysema, panic attacks, insomnia,
broncheostasis, ME (myalgic encephalitis), fatigue,
MS, sinusitis, snoring, high blood pressure,
agoraphobia, and problems of the immune system.

● WHO CAN'T BE TREATED?

In the hands of a professionally qualified
practitioner it can be used to treat most people as
the practitioner will modify the treatment
according to your needs.

● WHAT HAPPENS AT A CONSULTATION

Before your first appointment you will be sent an
extensive medical questionnaire to fill in.
Treatment is mostly conducted in weekend courses
in groups of five or six, usually no more than nine.
The course begins with a general introduction to
breathing, asthma, and the Buteyko method.

To assess your level of control over your breathing you'll be asked to do a three-step test called the control pause. You will then be taught a series of breathing exercises, including how to keep your nose unblocked and how to breathe through your nose. Practitioners aim to work alongside your GP so that once you have mastered the technique you'll be able to work with your doctor to reduce the levels of any medication you're taking.

Chi-gung

See QIGONG

Chinese herbalism

Chinese herbalism is part of the total health system of traditional Chinese medicine (TCM) and together with acupuncture it makes up the bulk of Chinese medical treatment, with most practitioners using both herbalism and acupuncture as complementary methods of treatment.

Chinese herbalists see good health as a harmonious balance between four key concepts as follows:

Yin and yang are complementary but opposing forces that govern every one of us. When they are in balance you feel well and healthy, but an imbalance can lead to ill health.

The 'eight principles' incorporate the forces of yin and yang and further sub-divide them into cold and heat, internal and external, deficiency and excess. These principles apply to every part of your body, and as long as they remain in balance you stay healthy.

Chi is the energy that flows around the body and binds the forces of yin and yang together. It travels through channels called meridians and when it flows freely the whole person is in balance, but if the flow becomes stagnant, blocked or has an imbalance, illness can result. As with acupuncture, Chinese herbalism aims to encourage the smooth flow of *chi* and restore harmony to the whole person.

Each of the five elements – **fire, earth, water, metal and wood** – is related to the organs in the body and the emotions. When *chi* flows easily between the elements they stay in balance, but if one of the elements is disrupted it can hamper the flow of *chi* which can, in turn, lead to physical or emotional ill health.

The Chinese herbalist's job is to identify any patterns of disharmony in the body and to prescribe herbal remedies to rebalance the various forces and strengthen and nourish the body.

● CONDITIONS TREATED

Eczema and other skin conditions, migraine, premenstrual syndrome and other women's health problems, fatigue, and digestive disorders such as irritable bowel syndrome.

● WHO CAN'T BE TREATED?

Remedies are usually suitable for anyone as long as they have been prescribed by a qualified Chinese herbalist; however, self-treatment with ready-made patent remedies for minor ailments is not recommended.

● WHAT HAPPENS AT A CONSULTATION

The therapist will assess your health using a system called the 'four examinations' as follows:

First the practitioner will look at your general appearance, paying particular attention to the colour, coating and condition of your tongue; the next stage involves listening to the sound of your voice and smelling your odour; the third examination involves asking questions about your lifestyle, health and medical history; and finally the fourth stage is touching any painful areas, or your skin if you have a rash, and most importantly taking your pulses, from three positions on each wrist.

The examination takes about an hour, after which the practitioner will decide on a remedy that matches your particular pattern of disharmony. Remedies are usually prescribed as herbal teas, but can also be given as pills, powders, pastes, ointments, creams and lotions. You may be given your remedy at the end of your consultation or you may be asked to return a week later to collect it. Any follow-up sessions with the herbalist will last about an hour.

Choosing a practitioner
Contact the Register of Chinese Herbal Medicine, PO Box 400, Wembley, Middlesex HA9 9NE
Tel. 020 7470 8740

Chiropractic

The word chiropractic originates from the Greek *cheiro*, meaning 'hand', and *praktos*, meaning 'to use'. The chiropractic method was developed in 1895 by a Canadian healer, Daniel D Palmer, who was fascinated by how bodies work. He first used chiropractic to cure the hearing of the janitor of his building, whose deafness had been caused by a back injury 17 years earlier. At the time Palmer was ridiculed by the medical establishment, but today chiropractic is one of the largest healthcare professions in the world.

Chiropractors believe that the spine is the key element of the body structure and that it plays a vital role in protecting the nervous system. As such, any spinal misalignment not only leads to back pain, but also affects the functioning of the whole body. A chiropractor treats the musculo-skeletal system – the bones, joints, muscles, ligaments and tendons – using a series of manipulative techniques.

● CONDITIONS TREATED

Neck, shoulder and back pain. Manipulation of the musculo-skeletal system may also relieve headaches, migraine, indigestion, constipation and asthma.

● WHO CAN'T BE TREATED?

A chiropractor will not treat broken bones or people with diseases such as rheumatoid arthritis and bone cancer; otherwise it's suitable for all, from newborn babies with colic to pregnant women with back pain.

● WHAT HAPPENS AT A CONSULTATION

The initial appointment usually takes about 30-45 minutes, at the beginning of which the therapist will take down the details of your medical history. You should tell her about any health problems, previous injury or past surgery as well as any current symptoms. She will then examine you. You'll be given a treatment gown and asked to strip to your underwear. Tests include taking your pulse and blood pressure and checking reflexes.

Choosing a practitioner
Contact the British Chiropractic Association, Blagrave House, 17 Blagrave Street, Reading RG1 1QB Tel. 0118 950 5950

She will also examine the alignment of your spine when you sit, stand, lie down and walk, and analyse individual joints and how they function. The chiropractor will probably X-ray your spine as this can help to reveal the extent of damage.

Clinical ecology

Clinical ecology (also known as environmental medicine) is a branch of medicine that developed from research into allergies, and although it is a fairly new discipline, abnormal reactions to food were already noted in ancient Greece by Hippocrates. In 1906 a Viennese paediatrician Baron Clemens von Piquet first used the term allergy to describe the way some of his patients reacted to certain foods or pollen. In the 1940s Dr Theron Randolph, an American allergy specialist, argued that sensitivity to everyday foods not only caused symptoms such as headaches and arthritis but that chemicals in the environment could have a hugely destructive effect on a person's health.

● CONDITIONS TREATED

Asthma, hay fever, headaches, migraines, digestive conditions, water retention, depression, fatigue, rheumatoid arthritis, eczema, psoriasis and recurrent infections.

● WHO CAN'T BE TREATED?

It is suitable for people of all ages and levels of fitness, as long as a professionally qualified practitioner is consulted.

● WHAT HAPPENS AT A CONSULTATION

The therapist will ask about your lifestyle, diet and medical history. He will then look for signs of sensitivity, such as swollen glands. A range of tests may be called on to identify the cause of the allergy, including a hair or blood test, and skin-prick tests where minute and diluted amounts of the suspected allergen are applied to an area of scratched skin.

The best treatment for allergies is avoidance. However, as this is not always practical, your practitioner may decide to desensitise you so that your body can cope with limited exposure to the allergen. This may be achieved through an elimination diet, which involves cutting out the suspect food or foods for up to 14 days then reintroducing them a week or so later to see if the symptoms return.

Alternatively a treatment called provocation neutralisation may be used, in which increasingly smaller concentrations of the irritant are given over a number of days. The point at which a reaction is not caused is seen as the neutralising dose and this is then taken as medicine twice daily.

It may be useful if you keep a food diary over this period listing everything you eat and when symptoms occur. This will provide useful information for your practitioner at any follow-up sessions that are required.

Choosing a practitioner
Contact the British Society for Allergy, Environmental and Nutritional Medicine, PO Box 7, Knighton LB7 1WT
Tel. 02380 812124

Colonic irrigation

The Egyptians practised bowel cleansing as long ago as 1500 BC – yet it is still regarded by most people as something new and slightly wacky. Colonic irrigation (or colonic hydrotherapy) is a detoxification process used to support and enhance the efficacy of other therapies. Practitioners are usually qualified in another therapy, often nutrition or herbalism, which they use in conjunction with colonics.

Treatment involves flushing out the colon with purified water to which vitamins, minerals, herbs, or homeopathic remedies may be added. The water sweeps away any faecal matter and toxins which may have accumulated and the supplements and remedies added to the water are more readily absorbed through the colon than when taken orally.

- ## CONDITIONS TREATED

    Mainly digestive disorders such as constipation, colitis, irritable bowel syndrome. It is also used for detoxification.

● WHO CAN'T BE TREATED?

It is suitable for most adults, but children should only be treated in exceptional circumstances.

● WHAT HAPPENS AT A CONSULTATION

The initial session will probably last an hour and a half, 50 minutes of which is taken up by the colonic treatment itself. After a full case history has been taken you will be asked to change into a gown with an opening at the back. You will then lie on a table and the therapist will insert a tube into your rectum.

When the water passes into your bowel, you will be asked to hold it for as long as this feels comfortable – usually between 15 seconds and two minutes. The therapist then releases the pressure and the water and accumulated matter flow down an outlet pipe into the drain.

This is repeated until either the therapist feels you have had enough or until the water runs clear.

Choosing a practitioner
For a list of practitioners, send an sae to the Colonic International Association,
16 Drummond Rick, Tring, Hertfordshire HP23 5DE
Tel. 01442 827687

Colour therapy

Colour therapy was pioneered in the 1940s by Swiss psychologist Dr Max Lüscher, when he found that a preference for one colour over another had physical and psychological implications. Colour therapists believe that everything in the world – including colours and the human body – vibrates at its own frequency. When you are in good health this frequency

remains constant, but the healthy vibration can be upset by illness. By choosing the colour that vibrates at the frequency needed to rebalance the body and by exposing patients to it for the appropriate length of time, the therapist can trigger the body's own healing process.

● CONDITIONS TREATED

Insomnia, asthma, depression, pain, anxiety and stress-related conditions. It can also help to speed up recovery after illness or surgery.

● **WHO CAN'T BE TREATED?**

As long as treatment is given by a professionally qualified practitioner just about anyone can be treated.

● **WHAT HAPPENS AT A CONSULTATION**

You'll be asked to complete a questionnaire about your medical history including any current health problems, emotional or physical. You will also be asked your favourite colours and the times of day that you feel you are at your best.

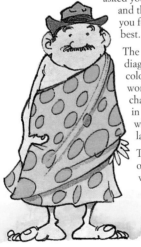

The therapist may diagnose you using a colour chart or may work with your aura and chakras (energy centres in the body) to see which colours you are lacking.

Treatment is carried out in a number of ways, all of which are aimed at providing your body with the colour it lacks. Therapists often shine a coloured light on those areas of the body that need treating. Some use a colour crystal torch, others drape coloured fabric around your body or they use the fabric with a lamp to flood the room with light in the required colour.

Some practitioners use their hands to detect and release areas of blocked energy and make you more receptive to the colour energy that they channel into your chakra.

At the end of the session, which can take up to two hours for a first appointment, the therapist will recommend that you wear certain colours, eat food in those colours, and visualise with the colours a few times a day. There are subsequent weekly sessions until your condition clears.

Choosing a practitioner
Contact the International Association for Colour Therapy, PO Box 3688, London SW13 0NX
Tel. 020 8878 5276

Counselling

See PSYCHOTHERAPY AND COUNSELLING

Craniosacral therapy

Craniosacral therapy was developed in the 1930s by an osteopath called William Sutherland. He noticed that cerebrospinal fluid (the clear liquid surrounding the brain and spinal cord) had an inherent rhythm rather like a tide ebbing and flowing through the body. He called this rhythm the 'breath of life', as it seemed to be influenced by the rate and depth of breathing. By gently manipulating the skull he found that he could alter this rhythmic flow which, he argued, might stimulate the body's self-healing ability and help cure conditions which may seem unrelated to the cranium.

● **CONDITIONS TREATED**

Arthritis, asthma, back pain, depression, digestive problems, premenstrual syndrome, sciatica, sports injuries and stress-related illnesses. It can also do much to improve quality of life in children with Down's syndrome, cerebral palsy and autism.

● **WHO CAN'T BE TREATED?**

Craniosacral therapy can be used on most people, even young children and babies.

● **WHAT HAPPENS AT A CONSULTATION**

A great deal of importance is attached to the first session which can last up to an hour and a half. The therapist will begin by taking a detailed history of your health and lifestyle. You will be asked to lie down for your treatment, although occasionally you may be asked to sit or stand to help release tension in particular joints and connective tissue. The practitioner will apply gentle pressure to your head and sometimes the base of your spine. Subsequent treatments last between 30 and 40 minutes.

Choosing a practitioner
Contact the Craniosacral Therapy Association,
The Upledger Institute UK, Marshall Place, Perth
PH2 8AH Tel. 01738 444404

Crystal and gemstone healing

For thousands of years crystals and gemstones have been attributed with healing and mystical powers. Today their unique vibrations and capacity to absorb, store and emit electromagnetic energy makes them a useful tool for a growing number of specially trained crystal therapists and other alternative practitioners such as spiritual healers.

Therapists believe that vital energy, the force that brings everything to life, travels through your body in channels called meridians, and that you are enveloped in a field of energy called an aura. Negative, destructive thoughts, stress, poor diet or radiation from computer screens can create an imbalance in the energy flow.

Crystals and gemstones come in various forms, and each has its own specific energy that vibrates at a certain level. While therapists use crystals and gemstones to treat the person as a whole and not just specific symptoms, certain crystals and gemstones are attributed with specific properties: amber is said to be calming, moonstone helps emotional and hormonal balance, and quartz is believed to boost healing.

● CONDITIONS TREATED

Stress, back pain, arthritis, wound healing. It can also help to boost your energy and spirit.

● WHO CAN'T BE TREATED?

Crystal and gemstone healing is suitable for most people, but babies and pregnant women are treated with special care.

● WHAT HAPPENS AT A CONSULTATION

The initial meeting will begin with a discussion about your health and lifestyle. Each practitioner uses crystals in different ways: some put crystals around your chair or treatment couch, thus surrounding you

Choosing a practitioner
Contact the Affiliation of Crystal Healing Organisations, 46 Lower Green Road, Esher, Surrey KT10 8HD
Tel. 020 8398 7252

with healing energy, while others place them on the chakras (specific sites on your body also called energy centres). You might be asked to hold a crystal in your hand, or if you are in pain the therapist may put a crystal on the painful area. The experience is a very calming and relaxing one as your own healing energies are reactivated and enhanced.

Dance movement therapy

Dance movement therapy was developed in the USA in the 1940s. Therapists believe that everyone has their own way of moving and that they unconsciously express themselves through their body language. Practitioners use dance and movement techniques to access the subconscious mind and to allow repressed emotions to be expressed non-verbally and subsequently to be accepted by the conscious self.

● CONDITIONS TREATED

Psychological and emotional problems.

● WHO CAN'T BE TREATED?

It is suitable for people of all ages and levels of fitness, including those with serious physical and mental disabilities.

● **WHAT HAPPENS AT A CONSULTATION**

You'll be taught on either a one-to-one or group basis. Before the treatment starts, you'll meet your therapist for an individual assessment.

You'll be asked to describe your emotional problems, lifestyle and work to enable the therapist to build a detailed picture of your life and relationships. She will also want to know what you hope to get out of the treatment.

Your session will start with a warm-up. The practitioner may or may not play music, as rhythm can be made with your hands, feet or legs, and she will assess how you express yourself with your body. Group therapy allows the practitioner to assess how the group as a whole works together and reacts to different situations. She will also have various items of equipment such as balls and bean bags that can be used as props to explore particular themes.

Choosing a practitioner
Contact the Association for Dance Movement Therapy, c/o Arts Therapies Department, Springfield Hospital, 61 Glenburnie Road, Tooting Bec, London SW17 7DJ
Tel. 020 8682 6236

Drama therapy

Drama can provide a powerful arena for self-expression. Practitioners believe that it can be used to access the subconscious mind and to explore even those experiences that took place before you could talk. Different role plays are used to encourage creativity, imagination and learning and self-awareness. The aim is to create a space in which you feel safe to examine your beliefs, feelings and attitudes, and to experiment with new ways of conducting yourself in the world.

● CONDITIONS TREATED

It can be used to treat a wide range of psychological and emotional problems, and to improve relationships between couples or within the family.

● WHO CAN'T BE TREATED?

It is suitable for most people in the hands of a professionally qualified therapist.

● WHAT HAPPENS AT A CONSULTATION

The therapy sessions may take place on either a one-to-one or group basis. Adult sessions usually last an hour and children's about half an hour. Before treatment begins you will meet your therapist for an assessment during which she will want to discuss your problems and what you hope to gain from the treatment. She will also ask about your lifestyle and relationships both now and in the past. This meeting is also a time for you to ask questions and air any concerns you may have. Therapists use different forms of drama to explore and reflect on feelings and relationships. Role play is also used to examine social situations in which you may feel unconfident. The therapist will encourage you to let go of memories and express hidden emotions in order to develop a better understanding of yourself and others.

Choosing a practitioner
Contact the British Association of Dramatherapists,
5 Sunnydale Villas, Durlston Road, Swanage,
Dorset BH19 2HY
Tel. 01929 555017 or 020 7731 0160

Dreamwork

In recent years lucid dreaming has come to be recognised as a powerful form of therapy. Lucid dreaming means being able to enter your dreams in a semi-conscious state and to control what happens in them. Some people already have this ability, while others can learn it. Practitioners believe almost anyone can summon up events, characters, and images into their dreams to improve their waking life. They also believe that lucid dreams are a useful way of tapping into the immune system: by dreaming lucidly about healthy cells replacing unhealthy ones, or by dreaming that you see yourself strong and well it may contribute to healing.

● CONDITIONS TREATED

Post-traumatic stress disorder, phobias.

● WHO CAN'T BE TREATED?

Dreamwork is not suitable for those who find it
hard to distinguish between waking and sleeping
reality, such as young children or anyone who is
psychotic.

● WHAT HAPPENS AT A CONSULTATION

The practitioner will discuss any problems you
have, whether you experience any recurring
dreams, and what you hope to gain from the
treatment. The first step in working with your
dreams is good dream recall. If you have trouble
remembering your dreams, the therapist will give
you tips on how to become aware that you are
dreaming and how to control them. You will be
advised to keep a dream diary or a dream
sketchbook. Your therapist may focus on the
themes that emerge from your dream diary or on
powerful individual dreams. Her aim will be to
help you uncover the meaning of your dreams and
so provide you with self-insight, rather than
imposing her own interpretation of your dreams
on you.

Choosing a practitioner
Contact the United Kingdom Council for
Psychotherapy, 167-169 Great Portland Street,
London W1N 5FB Tel. 020 7436 3002

Electrocrystal therapy

This is a system of healing in which electromagnetic fields are beamed at a patient, using crystals, to facilitate healing. It was originally developed by an ex-science teacher, Harry Oldfield, who found that he could detect illness and disease patterns using a special technique known as Kirlian photography. He then went on to develop a more sophisticated system of diagnosis and treatment. Oldfield found that if disease showed up as an imbalance in the body's energy field, then by directing a correcting vibrational pattern back to the body a harmonious balance would be restored. Treatment remains effective as long as patients do not go back to their old ways of mistreating their body with poor diets and stressful lifestyles.

● **CONDITIONS TREATED**

Therapists claim that electro-crystal therapy can help to balance almost every disease.

● WHO CAN'T BE TREATED?

It can be used by most people, even children.

● WHAT HAPPENS AT A CONSULTATION

The session starts with the therapist moving a meter that reads sound waves around your body to tune in to your own vibration. Any imbalance will be noted. You will then be asked to undress to your underwear and an instrument called a PIP scans your body. The result will be displayed on a computer monitor. You'll be able to see your body shape and also bands of colour representing your meridians.

The therapist's skill lies in the interpretation of this picture and she will be looking for energy centres that may be weak or blocked. She will then decide which areas need balancing and how much energy your body needs to correct the problem. You'll be asked to sit in a chair and hooked up to a machine with a rod placed over the thymus area of the brain and a headband filled with crystals on your head. The treatment is painless and sessions last for about an hour.

Choosing a practitioner
Contact the Yantra Centre for Vibrational Therapy, 204 Kensington Park Road, London W11 1NR
Tel. 020 7229 4781

Environmental medicine

See CLINICAL ECOLOGY

Eye Movement Desensitisation and Reprocessing Therapy (EMDR)

The use of eye movement to treat specific traumas can be traced back to the pendulum work of the early hypnotherapists, who used a watch or pencil to capture attention and direct eye movements. EMDR as a therapy, however, was developed in the late 1980s by Dr Francine Shapiro, then a research fellow at the Institute of Mental Research in California. She became interested in using eye movements to help people deal with (or reprocess) disturbing thoughts and memories when she noticed that she was able to reduce the intensity of thoughts that had been troubling her for some time when she moved her eyes in an upward diagonal direction. From this she developed a series of experiments aimed at harnessing eye movements as a means of dealing with difficult memories.

Practitioners believe that the effects of EMDR are very similar to the process that occurs during the period of dream sleep known as rapid eye movement (REM). The purpose of these naturally occurring movements, it seems, is to help your body reprocess or work through distressing self-destructive memories before stowing them away in the back of your mind where they can't disturb you.

● CONDITIONS TREATED

Post-traumatic stress disorder, phobias, grief, low self-esteem.

● WHO CAN'T BE TREATED?

In the hands of a professionally qualified therapist, EMDR is suitable for most people.

● WHAT HAPPENS AT A CONSULTATION

Sessions typically last about an hour. To start with, a thorough case history is taken. For the treatment you will be asked to bring to mind an image of a troubling event and to identify any feelings that may be linked with that memory. The therapist will hold her fingers in your line of vision and move them rapidly, and will ask you to focus on them. After you have been guided through several sets of movements the therapist will then ask you to describe what you're feeling and the image you're visualising. Often a new image appears which will have to be dealt with by the therapist as it forms a part of your memory network; each new image will be addressed as it arises until there are no more new images.

Therapists believe that getting you to focus on the difficult memory while at the same time focusing on her rapidly moving fingers literally moves blocked information along your information processing system and speeds up the healing process.

Choosing a practitioner
Contact EMDR UK, 1 Fairfield Avenue, Edgware, Middlesex HA8 9AG; send an sae for the practitioner list.

Faith healing

See HEALING (SPIRITUAL)

Fasting

Since ancient times fasting has been used as a means of healing. Records show that Hippocrates, the father of modern medicine, used fasts as part of his healing regime. It involves the avoidance – total or partial – of food and liquid except for pure water, for a specified period of time. Fasting does not mean starvation because most people have enough reserved food to last them for days if not weeks. In a controlled therapeutic fast (as used by naturopaths and ayurvedic practitioners) the body does not use any of its essential tissue as energy but uses its fat stores instead. At the same time it gives your digestive system a rest, detoxifies your system and encourages repair processes which help to restore and maintain good health. Naturopaths believe that most people would benefit from a fast one day a month even when healthy.

● CONDITIONS TREATED

Psoriasis, eczema, ulcerative colitis, Crohn's disease, asthma, heart disease, high blood pressure, auto-immune diseases such as lupus and rheumatoid arthritis.

● WHO CAN'T BE TREATED?

Long fasts (more than 48 hours) should only be undertaken with medical supervision and should be avoided by menstruating, pregnant and breastfeeding women, anyone who is seriously underweight, type 1 diabetics, children, anyone who is suffering from kidney failure, liver disease, severe anaemia, or who is taking prescription drugs.

● WHAT HAPPENS AT A CONSULTATION

Before treatment starts, your therapist (whether a naturopath or ayurvedic practitioner) will want to build a detailed picture of your medical history, as well as any current problems, your lifestyle, your job and how it affects you, plus your relationships with family, friends, and colleagues. Fasts are usually advocated for one, three,

Choosing a practitioner
Contact the General Council and Register of Naturopaths, Goswell House, 2 Goswell Road, Street, Somerset BA16 0JG
Tel. 01458 840072

five or seven days. In some cases it may be even longer. Before recommending a longer fast a naturopath will carry out a number of tests to ensure that your body will be able to withstand the effects. She will explain not only how to prepare yourself mentally and physically for a fast, but also the kind of side-effects you might experience, and how to end your fast safely.

See also AYURVEDA, NATUROPATHY

Feldenkrais

Feldenkrais is a system developed by a Russian-born doctor, Moshe Feldenkrais (1904-1984). A passionate judo player – he was the first European to become a black belt – he was plagued by a persistent knee injury and, determined to find a cure for it, he began to study body movement and posture. He found that most people tend to use their bodies inefficiently, usually resulting in long-term problems such as reduced flexibility, bad breathing habits, poor co-ordination and joint or muscular pain. Feldenkrais held that by learning how to use the body's framework correctly these problems could be cleared or improved.

His method is more a learning process than a therapy, and it helps you to understand your body and what may be causing a particular problem. It teaches you to explore the way you move so that your body can

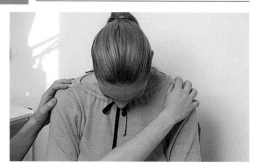

correct itself and adapt to find the most comfortable movements. It encourages easy, graceful movements, better breathing habits and relaxation.

● CONDITIONS TREATED

Sports injuries, back problems, shoulder and neck pain, arthritis, rheumatism and stroke-related problems such as poor mobility and flexibility.

● WHO CAN'T BE TREATED?

Feldenkrais is suitable for people of all ages and levels of fitness.

● WHAT HAPPENS AT A CONSULTATION

Feldenkrais is taught within group sessions (known as Awareness Through Movement) or in one-to-one sessions (called Functional Integration). Some students only attend the group sessions but individual lessons are sometimes offered when you start so that the teacher can assess you. The assessment is a hands-on one in which you are guided through a series of movements. The teacher will assess how you move, noting both stiff and flexible areas. You will be taught how to recognise habitual patterns, and how to replace them with more comfortable ways of using your body.

In group sessions students are talked through a series of gentle moves, often done lying down so that the body is always supported by the floor. Sessions begin with small movements, building up as the lesson progresses. The movements are slow and mindful. If you find any of the moves uncomfortable you'll be encouraged to visualise yourself performing them instead. The second approach used by practitioners is known as functional integration, where the therapist works on a one-to-one basis using touch and manipulation to address your specific needs.

Sessions are on a weekly basis to start with, after which you will be encouraged to attend a refresher every once in a while.

> **Choosing a practitioner**
> Contact The Feldenkrais Guild UK, PO Box 370, London NW10 3XA enclosing an SAE for a directory of Feldenkrais practitioners.

Feng shui

Feng shui is the ancient Chinese art and science of placement. The main concept behind feng shui is energy flow: feng shui is to your home what acupuncture is to your body. If the energy flow in your home is smooth and harmonious you will prosper. Feng shui practitioners regard the home as an extension of the body. Just as different organs have different functions, even different spaces in one room can have different functions, and everything has to be balanced.

Practitioners believe that you can radically change your life by changing the way in which you organise

and decorate your home. For example, if you're single and looking to settle down, take a good look at your home – if it says 'I am a single person', that is how you will stay. If you are not sleeping well at night, it may be because your bed is in a position that makes it difficult for you to relax.

● CONDITIONS TREATED

Feng shui can clear areas of your life in which you feel you have become stuck, and resolve recurring emotional and relationship problems.

● WHO CAN'T BE TREATED?

Every home can be treated, for even if structural changes can't be made practitioners have a wide range of 'cures' to harmonise the flow of energy.

● WHAT HAPPENS AT A CONSULTATION

A feng shui practitioner will usually visit you in your own home. The length of the session will depend on the size of your home, but one to two hours might be expected. The practitioner will ask you about any areas of your personal life or work that you feel to be problematic, and will form a detailed assessment of each room in the house. After the appointment she will send you a report with suggested changes.

The job of the practitioner is to create the most harmonious energy flow possible within your home or workplace. The main obstacle to this is clutter. If your home is filled with piles of old papers and magazines, overflowing drawers, and surfaces covered with bric-a-brac, the first thing you'll be advised to do is get rid of all the clutter. Most people find this very liberating.

She may make suggestions regarding a new colour scheme or moving furniture, plants and ornaments. She will also make use of 'cures,' such as mirrors and crystals, to boost the energy flow in your home. Any additional questions you may have can be dealt with by telephoning the practitioner.

Consultations by post can also be arranged if you send the practitioner a floorplan of your home or workplace.

Choosing a practitioner
Contact Feng Shui Network International, PO Box 2133, London W1A 1RL Tel. 07000 336474

See also GEOPATHIC THERAPY

Flotation therapy

Flotation therapy was developed in America from the work of Dr John C. Lilly, who was also trained as a psychoanalyst and specialist in neurophysiology. In the 1950s be began research into how the brain reacted when denied external stimulation. He carried out experiments in the soundproof chambers used by the Navy to train its divers, the aim of which was to place the divers under stress, but instead their stress levels plummeted. He found that isolating the body and mind from external stimuli induced a state of deep relaxation in the participants. Lilly then went on to develop his own tank which he called a sensory deprivation chamber.

In the 1970s Lilly's chambers were renamed flotation tanks when their ability to promote deep relaxation was recognised. Floating seems to stimulate the body to produce endorphins, which act as natural painkillers, and it also stimulates the right side of the brain, promoting creativity.

● CONDITIONS TREATED

Stress, anxiety, ulcers, high blood pressure, headaches, migraine, addictions, heart disease, back pain, tired muscles. Flotation therapy can also boost the immune system.

● WHO CAN'T BE TREATED?

Anyone with open or inflamed skin conditions should not go into the tank. Flotation therapy is also not recommended for children or anyone with a history of psychosis. If you are claustrophobic you must be professionally supervised.

● WHAT HAPPENS AT A CONSULTATION

Flotation tanks are usually installed in health clubs or float centres. The soundproofed tanks measure about 2.5m (8ft) long and 1.25m (4ft) wide and contain just 25cm (10in) of water kept at skin temperature and with enough salts and minerals dissolved in it to enable you to float.

The therapist will explain the procedure to you and give you earplugs to use in the tank. You will be

Choosing a practitioner
Contact the Float Tank
Association, PO Box
11024, London SW4 72F
Tel. 020 7627 4962

left to undress (you may
float naked, or change
into a swimming
costume) and get into
the tank. The float takes
place in complete or
semi-darkness but you
may switch on the light or open the door whenever
you feel the need. Some tanks are also equipped
with two-way microphones to allow you to talk to
your practitioner.

Sessions last for about an hour to an hour and a
half.

Flower and gem remedies

The ancient Egyptians and Africans used flowers to
control emotional states and imbalances, as did the
16th-century
European
healer
Paracelsus. Today
flower remedies are still
a popular remedy for
emotional problems, the best-
known being those created by
Dr Edward Bach (pronounced *Batch*),
although others may be found

worldwide, in the USA, Hawaii, the Himalayas, Africa, the Amazon and New Zealand. Gem essences too are now available, made by steeping precious and semi-precious stones in spring water.

Flower and gem essences are thought to retain the energy of the substances from which they were made. This energy seems to work on a vibrational level within the body, stimulating its natural healing mechanisms into action.

● CONDITIONS TREATED

Negative emotional states, such as anxiety, fearfulness, loneliness and despair.

● WHO CAN'T BE TREATED?

They are suitable for anyone from babies to the elderly; even animals and plants can benefit.

● WHAT HAPPENS AT A CONSULTATION

Dr Bach designed his remedies so that people could treat themselves, but many practitioners, such as herbalists and homeopaths, use them in certain cases, and some therapists work with flower and gem remedies exclusively.

A consultation should begin with a discussion about why you have come to see the practitioner. While listening to you, she will also take note of your posture, appearance, and tone of voice as these can reveal a lot about your emotional state. To enable her to select the right remedy the therapist will not only want to know what problems you have at home or at work but also how you feel about and react to them. At the end of the consultation she will prescribe one or a number of remedies depending on your needs.

Choosing a practitioner
Contact the Dr Edward Bach Centre, Mount Vernon, Sotwell, Wallingford, Oxfordshire OX10 0PZ
Tel. 01491 834678
or the Flower Essence Repertoire, The Living Tree, Milland, Liphook, Hants GU30 7JS
Tel. 01428 741672

Geomancy

See GEOPATHIC THERAPY

Geopathic therapy

Sometimes referred to as geomancy, geopathic therapy is a method of divination drawn from different theories about the ways in which the environment may have damaging effects on health. This idea is not a new one and cultures as old as the Australian Aborigines and the Chinese have long believed in invisible energy pathways. The increasingly popular practice of Feng Shui is a type of geomancy.

● CONDITIONS TREATED

Anxiety, depression, insomnia, fatigue, headaches, migraine, rheumatoid arthritis.

● WHO CAN'T BE TREATED?

Geopathic therapy is suitable for people of all ages and levels of fitness, provided a qualified practitioner is consulted. It is important to tell both your practitioner and your doctor if you are pregnant or trying to conceive.

Choosing a practitioner
Contact Healthy Home Consultants, Healthy Home, PO Box 249, Keithley, Yorkshire B220 8YN
Tel. 07000 336474

● WHAT HAPPENS AT A CONSULTATION

The practitioner will usually visit you in your own home and, depending on the size of your home, a session may last for up to two hours.

Some practitioners believe that negative energy or 'geopathic stress' is created by underground streams, geological faults, and manmade features, such as power cables. A practitioner may use dowsing to pinpoint areas of negative energy and will try to rebalance it by moving furniture or 'soaking up' harmful energy with crystals.

See also FENG SHUI

Gestalt therapy

The word *gestalt* is German for whole, and this reflects the central principles of this therapy: that all neurosis originates in unnatural splits either within yourself or in your relation to the world around you. It was developed by a Fritz Perls, who emigrated from Nazi Germany to the west coast of America. He believed that we are all basically healthy beings and have the ability to know what is best for ourselves if we just learn to listen to our bodies and instincts rather than splitting away from their messages. And crucial to the healing process is integration of the person as a whole.

Gestalt is a very practical approach with practitioners focusing on how you get yourself into difficulties, not why. Perls noticed that people tend to repeat certain patterns of behaviour throughout their lives.

He believed that only by becoming aware of those patterns can you begin to change them.

● CONDITIONS TREATED

Emotional problems.

● WHO CAN'T BE TREATED?

It is suitable for most adults.

● WHAT HAPPENS AT A CONSULTATION

The therapist will want to know why you've come to see her. She won't say much but will ask gently probing questions to get you talking so that she can become familiar with you, observe and learn. As the sessions progress the therapist will use a variety of practical techniques, such as imagining yourself as a cushion on an empty chair with whom you talk through your feelings and act out old arguments. Don't expect your therapist to furnish you with answers, though. Her main aim is to help you to come up with your own solutions rather than telling you what is wrong.

Choosing a practitioner
Contact the United Kingdom Council for Psychotherapy, 167–169 Great Portland Street, London W1N 5FB Tel. 020 7436 3002

Healing (spiritual)

The practice of healing, sometimes referred to as the laying on of hands, is one of the oldest therapies and was used by the ancient Egyptian, Chinese and Greek civilisations as a means of treating disease. In the Middle Ages, healers were viewed with suspicion by the Christian Church and many were branded as witches and put to death. As a result spiritual healing was restricted to the clergy. It wasn't until the middle of the last century that healers such as Harry Edwards began to reclaim spiritual healing as a lay skill and its popularity soared.

Today healing is practised in hospitals, pain clinics and cancer units. Practitioners regard themselves as a channel through which healing energy is delivered to the patient. When a healer lays her hands on you she acts as a conductor for the energy which she believes has the intelligence to go where it is needed and trigger your body's own healing mechanism into action.

Other methods of healing include REIKI and THERAPEUTIC TOUCH, plus:

Aura healing: practitioners claim to see bands of colour around the patient that represent their state of health. They place their hands on or near the patient and visualise the healing colour they need.

Faith healing: the patient is required to believe in the power of the healer or the deity the healer claims to represent for a cure to take place.

Distant healing: healers visualise healing energy being transmitted from them to the distant client.

Shamanism: healers go into a trance-like state in which they claim to be able to determine the cause of illness and learn how to treat it.

● CONDITIONS TREATED

Spiritual healing can help with all health problems – physical, mental or emotional – but it does seem to be particularly effective on conditions such as frozen shoulder, arthritis and bad backs. An important part of healing is helping people with terminal illnesses to pass away peacefully.

● WHO CAN'T BE TREATED?

Spiritual healing can help anyone, but whether it does or not can't be guaranteed. It should not be used on women during labour or for ten days after, nor on children under 18 unless their parent or guardian has sought medical help and given their consent for healing.

● WHAT HAPPENS AT A CONSULTATION

Healing sessions can be conducted on a one-to-one or a group basis, and may take place in a church, a centre or clinic, or at your own or your

practitioner's home. You will be asked some general questions about the problems you are having, whether physical, emotional or spiritual, your medical history and lifestyle.

For the treatment you will either be asked to lie on a treatment couch or to remain seated. The practitioner will start by attuning herself to the healing energy. She may assess your body's energy levels

Choosing a practitioner
Contact the Confederation of Healing
Organisations, Suite J, 2nd Floor, The Red and
White House, 113 High Street, Berkhamsted,
Hertfordshire HP4 2DJ Tel. 01442 870660; or The
National Federation of Spiritual Healers, Old Manor
Farm Studio, Church Street, Sunbury-on-Thames,
Middlesex TW16 6RG Tel. 0891 616080

with her hands held just above you. A session can last
from a few minutes to an hour, depending on what
your body needs.

Hellerwork

Hellerwork was developed in the United States in
1978 by Joseph Heller. An aerospace engineer, he
applied engineering principles to the human body to
develop a system of treatment similar to that used in
ROLFING. He believed that if your body is structurally
misaligned every movement you make will cause stress
to your body.

Misalignment can stem from a number of factors
including bad posture and emotional stress. If you
twist your ankle, for example, your body will respond
by holding itself in a different way even after the injury
has cleared up, and Hellerwork practitioners believe
that emotional hurt affects you in the same fashion, by

holding it in your muscles. Hellerworkers aim to realign the body and unblock the physical and emotional patterns responsible for its misalignment, by combining massage with exercise.

● CONDITIONS TREATED

Hellerwork aims not only to treat disease but to prevent it. Conditions that respond well to it include back and neck pain, headaches and general aches and pains.

● WHO CAN'T BE TREATED?

Hellerwork is not suitable for people with certain types of cancer. Otherwise, it can be tailored to suit the needs of most people, including pregnant women.

● WHAT HAPPENS AT A CONSULTATION

The full course is made up of a number of sessions of an hour and a half each. At the beginning of your initial visit the therapist will want to put together your full case history. She will take

---

Choosing a practitioner
Contact the European Hellerwork Association, c/o Roger Golten, The Ability Centre, 29 Crawford Street, London W1H 1PL Tel. 020 7723 5676
www.hellerwork.net

photographs both at the beginning and end of the course to show you how your posture has changed.

You will be advised not to eat for two hours before each session and for the treatment itself you will be asked to strip to your underwear. Hellerworkers use firm massage to release tension in your muscles, while engaging you in dialogue. They focus first on realigning and freeing tension in the body, then on working on core muscles which are often underused, such as the pelvic floor, and finally on improving your body's overall movement and balance. Some of the work may hurt slightly, but most people find it bearable and often describe it as 'good pain'.

Herbalism (Western)

Since ancient times herbs have been used in Greece, Rome, Egypt, India, China and Persia for their medicinal properties. For a while, around the 18th century, our own Western tradition of herbalism fell out of favour but it is now popular again.

The main aim of herbalism is to strengthen the body's systems so that it is better equipped to heal itself and to fight disease before it takes hold.

- ## CONDITIONS TREATED

Most illnesses, including migraine, arthritis, insomnia, cystitis, eczema, irritable bowel syndrome, premenstrual syndrome and menopausal problems.

- ## WHO CAN'T BE TREATED?

Herbalism is suitable for everyone from babies and young children to pregnant women and the elderly, but anyone who is taking prescribed drugs should let their GP know that they are seeing a herbalist (and vice versa).

● WHAT HAPPENS AT A CONSULTATION

Your first appointment with a herbalist may take an hour or so. The practitioner will want to build a complete picture of you and all your problems, not just the most pressing ones, to help her form her diagnosis. Medical herbalists receive medical training so are qualified to carry out a basic physical check-up, such as taking your blood pressure and pulse, and testing your reflexes. Once the examination is complete the herbalist will decide on the appropriate remedy or remedies. These are dispensed in a variety of forms including tablets, capsules, lotions and creams, as well as in liquid form as a tincture, infusion or decoction.

As well as prescribing herbs, a herbalist may well recommend changes to your diet and lifestyle and offer advice on how to reduce stress in your life.

Choosing a practitioner

Contact the International Register of Consultant Herbalists and Homoeopaths, 32 King Edwards Road, Swansea SA1 4LL Tel. 01792 655886; or the National Institute of Medical Herbalists, 56 Longbrook Street, Exeter, Devon EX4 6AH Tel. 01392 426022

Homeopathy

Homeopathy aims to help the body to heal itself by treating it as a whole, and not just the symptoms in question. The roots of homeopathy can be traced back to the 5th century BC and the writings of Hippocrates, the father of modern medicine. But it was the work of the German doctor and chemist Samuel Hahnemann in the late 18th century that brought homeopathy to prominence. Hahnemann used himself as a guinea pig and found that when he dosed himself with quinine, then used to fight malaria, he developed malaria-like symptoms even though he did not have the disease itself. He concluded that it was quinine's ability to cause malaria-like symptoms that made it so effective against the disease. Thus he developed his central premise of treating like with like, so that a substance that causes the symptoms of illness in a well person can be used to treat those symptoms in someone who is

ill. So, a homeopath would treat blocked sinuses, for example, with minute doses of a substance (a homeopathic remedy) that would actually cause blocked sinuses if given in a larger dose.

Homeopaths believe in a vital force – a healing power – that keeps the body in a state of health, and that the symptoms of disease or illness are a sign that the vital force is out of balance and that it is working to fight off disease and heal itself. As such, symptoms should not be suppressed but the body should be given help to heal itself. For this reason homeopathic remedies are aimed at stimulating the body's healing mechanism rather than suppressing symptoms.

● CONDITIONS TREATED

Because homeopaths treat the whole person and not the disease, homeopathy can be used to tackle just about everything. However conditions that seem to respond particularly well to it include: asthma, eczema, psoriasis, allergies, anxiety, nervous tension, shock, menstrual and menopausal problems, colds, constipation, vomiting, diarrhoea, rheumatoid arthritis.

● WHO CAN'T BE TREATED?

Homeopathic remedies are safe for everyone including babies, pregnant women and the elderly. Some medical drugs can affect the efficacy of homeopathic remedies so be sure to let your therapist know of any medication you may be taking.

● WHAT HAPPENS AT A CONSULTATION

When you first visit a homeopath you'll be asked numerous questions about yourself and your lifestyle, your symptoms and medical history, your diet, whether you like sweet or salty food, whether you're a morning or evening person, your favourite time of year and so on. If your homeopath is also medically qualified she may give you a physical examination. All of this information will enable the homeopath to build a complete picture of you, and to select the appropriate remedy. You will probably only be given one remedy at a time, but the prescription may change as your symptoms change. They come in the form of lactose tablets, pills, powder or granules. They are made by diluting the substance in question many times. Each dilution is graded for potency either as c, x, or m. M is the most dilute and paradoxically the most potent.

Your first consultation will last between one and two hours; subsequent appointments are shorter.

Choosing a practitioner
Contact the Society of Homoeopaths, 2 Artisan Road, Northampton NN1 4HU Tel. 01604 621400.
For homeopaths who are also medical doctors contact: the British Homeopathic Association, 15 Clerkenwell Close, London EC1R 0AA
Tel. 020 7566 7800

Hydrotherapy

Hydrotherapy involves the use of water to cleanse and revitalise the body and maintain good health. Spas have been popular ever since Roman times both for leisure and as a healing tool. But the father of modern hydrotherapy is generally considered to be a 19th-century Bavarian monk, Father Sebastian Kneipp. He claimed that water could cure illness by helping the body get rid of waste products. He used a variety of methods including hot and cold baths, steam baths, showers and wraps, all of which are still in use today, with whirlpools and water jets having been added to the mix.

● **CONDITIONS TREATED**

Back pain, muscle aches and sprains, circulation problems, asthma, bronchitis, cystitis, menstrual problems, anxiety, stress, fatigue, headaches.

● **WHO CAN'T BE TREATED?**

Hot or moor baths, steam baths, and saunas should not be used if you suffer with high blood pressure, angina, or heart disease. Women in the first three months of pregnancy should avoid taking steam or sitz baths and for the rest of their pregnancy steam treatment should only be used for a maximum of ten minutes. Steam treatment should not be used by anyone who has epilepsy, asthma, or a history of thrombosis.

● **WHAT HAPPENS AT A CONSULTATION**

Your therapist will have a general discussion with you about your health problems, medical history, and lifestyle. This will enable her to select the best method of treatment to suit your needs, which may include some of the following:

Hot or cold compresses – towels previously soaked in hot or cold water and wrung out are applied to the affected part of the body. Hot compresses boost blood flow and cold compresses slow down blood flow.

High-powered jets – hot or cold water is fired on to your back. This is said to stimulate circulation.

Hot or warm baths – soaking for 20-30 minutes in hot or warm water to which oils, herbs, and minerals such as Epsom salts are added can help arthritic conditions and swollen joints, while relaxing muscles.

Moor bath – this potent herbal blend which looks like mud sludge is simply added to warm bath water and you soak in it for 20 minutes to aid sleep.

Sitz baths – this involves two hip baths placed side by side, one filled with hot water, and the other with cold water. You sit in one and place your feet in the other and alternate between the two. This is thought to help haemorrhoids, menstrual problems and cystitis.

Thalassotherapy – this involves the use of sea-water jets, seaweed wraps or sea-water baths to cleanse and tone the skin and aid relaxation.

Turkish baths or steam rooms or cabinets – you sit in a steamy room for about 20 minutes or in a cabinet for up to an hour to help with the elimination of impurities.

Saunas – you sit in a hot, dry room for 20 minutes to encourage sweating, which helps with the elimination of waste products.

- Wraps – this involves wrapping cold, wet flannel sheets around your body. These are then covered with dry towels and topped off with blankets. This encourages sweating and the elimination of waste products.

Choosing a practitioner
Contact Tyringham Naturopathic Clinic,
Newport Pagnell, Buckinghamshire MK16 9ER
Tel. 01908 610450
or General Council and Register of Naturopaths,
Goswell House, 2 Goswell Road, Street, Somerset
BA16 0JG Tel. 01458 840072

Hypnotherapy

One of the forefathers of hypnotherapy was an 18th-century Austrian doctor, Anton Mesmer (hence the word mesmerise). A stage hypnotist, he was also a healer and he successfully treated many people before being discredited by the French government. Despite this somewhat rocky start for hypnotherapy, there is now a wealth of scientific research to support it.

Hypnotherapy is a form of psychotherapy which works on the subconscious mind. Therapists use a range of simple techniques to induce hypnosis, a trance-like state in which your mind is much more open than

normal. The therapist then makes suggestions which you store in your mind to bring about therapeutic benefits.

● CONDITIONS TREATED

Habit problems such as insomnia, blushing, bedwetting, smoking, drinking and drug abuse, anorexia and overeating, and nailbiting. Also phobias, stress-related problems such as IBS (irritable bowel syndrome), eczema, and unresolved trauma.

● WHO CAN'T BE TREATED?

Children under the age of four are too young to co-operate with the therapist.

● WHAT HAPPENS AT A CONSULTATION

The first appointment will be an assessment session, where you and your practitioner get to know each other. The therapist will ask about your problem and why you have chosen hypnotherapy. This session is also a good time for you to ask questions. After the assessment which usually lasts between 60 and 90 minutes, the therapist may treat you, but often treatment won't begin until the second session. (The second and subsequent appointments last around an hour.)

You'll be asked to lie on a couch or sit in a comfortable chair. Once you are in trance-like state, the therapist will address your problem using carefully worded suggestions. Note that in this state, you can't be made to say or do anything that goes against your principles. At the end of each session the therapist will gently bring you back to consciousness.

Choosing a practitioner
Contact the National Register of Hypnotherapists and Psychotherapists, 12 Cross Street, Nelson, Lancashire BB9 7EN Tel. 01282 716839

Iridology

Iridology was developed in the 1800s by a Hungarian doctor, Ignatz von Peczeley. As a child, he was playing with an owl when he accidentally broke its foot and he noticed that a black mark appeared in the owl's eye. Years later, as a trained homeopath, he was treating a woman with a broken leg when he noticed a similar mark in her eye. He researched further and found that many signs of illness are registered in the iris, the coloured part of the eye.

Iridology is a method of assessing a person's health and susceptibility to disease by examining the structure, colour, and markings of the iris. The practice is less about actually diagnosing disease than pinpointing a person's tendency to ill-health and taking steps to prevent disease from developing.

● CONDITIONS TREATED

Iridology is used to diagnose conditions rather than treat illness. A practitioner should be able to tell, for example, if your pancreas is underfunctioning or if your digestion is sluggish. She could also pick up a genetic predisposition to problems such as heart disease.

● WHO CAN'T BE TREATED?

It is suitable for people of all ages and levels of fitness.

● WHAT HAPPENS AT A CONSULTATION

The first visit lasts for about an hour. The practitioner will look into your eyes using a small

torch and a magnifying glass. She may also use a video camera to record, then display your eyes on a TV screen. She may discuss any obvious signs she has spotted and then later draw up a detailed analysis for you to keep. At the end of the session you will be asked to fill in a health questionnaire which will provide additional information and help with recommending treatment. Iridologists often practise other therapies.

Choosing a practitioner
Guild of Naturopathic Iridologists, 94 Grosvenor Road, London SW1V 3LF Tel. 020 7834 3579.
International Association of Clinical Iridologists, 853 Finchley Road, London NW11 8LX.
Send an sae for practitioner list.

Laughter therapy

Psychoneuroimmunology (meaning the way in which the mind affects our physical state) is a new branch of research showing that just as negative emotions can bring about destructive chemical changes in the body and cause disease, positive emotions can be therapeutic. And we all know how good it feels to laugh! Recent studies show that people who regularly use laughter, humour and play as coping strategies for everyday events have a significantly higher count of the antibodies that fight disease. When you smile your facial muscles tighten and alter blood flow, decreasing the temperature of the brain's blood supply which is associated with good moods. Laughter also ventilates your lungs, and leaves your muscles, nerves, and heart warm and relaxed. It speeds up your heart rate and increases your oxygen intake.

● CONDITIONS TREATED

It boosts the immune system, hastens recovery from illness and fosters general good health.

● WHO CAN'T BE TREATED?

It is suitable for most people.

● WHAT HAPPENS AT A CONSULTATION

Laughter therapy is usually practised in group workshops. The UK's first laughter clinic was run by the pioneering healer Robert Holden. Patients are encouraged to act out a range of scenarios guaranteed to bring a smile to their faces, such as pretending to be a fish finger or

Choosing a practitioner
For details of Laughter Workshops send an sae to 34 Denwood Avenue, Handsworth, Birmingham N20 2AB

working with a partner to turn themselves into a piece of furniture. A system called transcendental chuckling is also used, involving playing a tape of a man starting to laugh. It begins with a little chuckle and finally explodes in a side-splitting belly laugh. It is impossible for those listening to it not to smile or grin in response.

Holden believes that adults don't laugh and play as much as they should and this has an ageing effect. Whereas children laugh an average of 150 times a day, adults only manage a poor six times.

Light therapy

We know from their earliest writings that the ancient Egyptians, Greeks, Romans and Arabs all understood the healing power of sunlight. Centuries later in 1903 the Danish doctor Niels Finsen won the Nobel Prize in Medicine for his work using ultraviolet light to treat tuberculosis.

Today light is used to regulate the body's biological clock, treat jaundice in premature babies, boost vitality, and is particularly important in the treatment of seasonal affective disorder, a condition thought to be caused by a lack of light during the winter months. Daylight also triggers the production of vitamin D, needed for the absorption of certain minerals such as calcium. Therapists claim that ultraviolet light has an antibacterial action which helps to clear skin conditions such as acne.

● CONDITIONS TREATED

Seasonal affective disorder (SAD), depression, skin conditions such as psoriasis, insomnia, premenstrual syndrome, infertility.

● WHO CAN'T BE TREATED?

It is suitable for everyone from young babies to the elderly.

● WHAT HAPPENS AT A CONSULTATION

The therapist will begin by taking a detailed medical history. Next you'll be asked to lie on a treatment couch. If you wear contact lenses or glasses you'll need to remove them as light can only reach the pineal glands, essential for hormone balance, through your eyes. For best results you'll be asked to keep your eyes open. The therapist will put you under a full-spectrum or bright white light. Treatment lasts up to an hour; you may be given a light box to use at home for 20 minutes a day.

Choosing a practitioner
Contact the SAD Association, PO Box 989, Steyning, West Sussex BN44 3HG
Tel. 01903 814942

McTimoney Chiropractic

This is an ultra gentle form of chiropractic developed by John McTimoney, a British chiropractor. He believed that the main cause of disease and pain is misalignment of the body's structure, which can occur in one area but affect the entire body.

The method of treatment is similar to ordinary CHIROPRACTIC, in that practitioners work on the structure of the body with emphasis on the spine and nervous system, but McTimoney practitioners use only their hands to manipulate the body.

● CONDITIONS TREATED

Musculo-skeletal problems, sciatica, sports injuries, headache, migraine, emotional problems.

● WHO CAN'T BE TREATED?

The technique is so gentle it is even suitable for babies and the elderly.

● WHAT HAPPENS AT A CONSULTATION

Practitioners take a full case history, assess your posture, check your spine and the angle of your pelvis, plus your arms, legs, hands, feet, thorax, and skull. If they think you need an X-ray, they will refer you back to your doctor or to a hospital.

Treatment involves using a high-speed thrust where the practitioner uses one hand as a 'hammer' and the other as a 'nail' to free the joints and ease tension in the surrounding muscle. This may sound painful but the treatment is actually extremely gentle.

Choosing a practitioner
Contact the McTimoney Chiropractic Association,
21 High Street, Eynsham, Oxon OX8 1HE
Tel. 01865 880974

Magnet therapy

The practice of using magnets to aid healing dates back as far as the ancient civilisations of Egypt, Greece, and China. Today it is very popular in Japan. Magnet therapy is also known as magnetotherapy or biomagnetic therapy.

The idea that the body depends on some kind of magnetic balance was reinforced when the first astronauts returned to earth feeling nauseous. The problem was solved by fitting magnets into their space suits to help the astronauts maintain their natural magnetic balance while in space.

Practitioners claim that in the same way as the earth has a natural magnetic field so do human body cells. But the influences of modern-day living and electro-pollution from appliances such as microwave ovens and televisions insulate you away from the earth's natural magnetism, causing your body to lose its magnetic balance.

According to practitioners, iron atoms in your red blood cells respond to magnetism so that when a magnet is placed on your body it improves blood flow in that area. Correct use of magnet therapy can improve general health and act on specific problems and has been shown to improve the supply of oxygen to cells, increase energy levels and accelerate the healing process. It also boosts the immune system and reduces inflammation, bruising and stiffness.

● CONDITIONS TREATED

Bone disorders, such as fractures and osteoporosis,
arthritis, inflamed joints and sprains, back and
neck pain, insomnia, headaches, migraine, fatigue,
hormonal and circulation problems.

● WHO CAN'T BE TREATED?

Pregnant women or those trying to conceive, and
anyone fitted with a pacemaker.

● WHAT HAPPENS AT A CONSULTATION

After a structural assessment the practitioner will
decide on how best to treat you. A variety of
methods is used and, depending on the type of
magnet worked with, a session can take a few
minutes or a few hours.

Types of magnetic treatment include:

Biomagnets – these are small magnets about the size of the end of a pencil. They are stuck on your acupuncture points to stimulate specific meridians (your body's energy pathways) and so channel your body's own magnetic force.

'Active' magnets – these are plugged into an electric circuit to produce a pulsing electro-magnetic field around the body. They are used by some physiotherapists and osteopaths for easing sprains and helping to repair damaged tissue and bones.

Magnetomax machine – this works by applying the correct polarity and strength of magnetic field.

Magnet therapy is often used as a self-help treatment using what are called 'static' magnets which emit a low electromagnetic field. Products which can be bought for home use include magnet shoe insoles, pillows, wrist watches, knee belts, necklaces, car seats, and mattresses.

Choosing a practitioner
British Biomagnetic Association,
31 St Marychurch Road, Torquay, Devon,
TQ1 3JF Tel. 01803 293346

Massage

Massage is one of the oldest therapies in the world: as long as 3,000 years ago the Greeks and Romans were using massage as a healthcare tool, and in the 19th century the Swedish gymnast, Per Henrik Ling, developed what we now call Swedish massage. But it was Austrian psychoanalyst Wilhelm Reich who made the connection between massage and emotions: he believed that unexpressed emotions such as anger are held in the body, and that the physical manipulation of the body can not only relieve tense and rigid muscles, it can also stimulate the release of pent-up emotions.

Massage combines the soothing properties of touch with the skilful manipulation of muscles, tendons and ligaments. This stimulates circulation and the nervous and digestive systems, eases stiff muscles and joints, increases energy, and releases emotional tension, gradually restoring the person back to full health.

Babies particularly benefit from massage. Soft strokes over the body help to reinforce the bonding process between parent and child, to soothe a fractious child and to reassure a sick one. Research shows that children sleep better when massaged regularly.

● CONDITIONS TREATED

Stress-related conditions, insomnia, depression, sports injuries, rheumatism, sciatica, digestive problems such as irritable bowel syndrome,

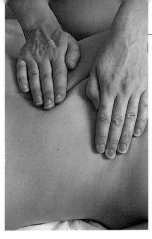

constipation, premenstrual syndrome and general aches and pains.

● WHO CAN'T BE TREATED?

Massage can be used to treat everyone from premature babies to the terminally ill. However you should tell your therapist if you have had surgery or cancer within the past 12 months, have recently broken a bone, had a strain or sprain, or are pregnant, as they will know which areas to avoid and which type of massage is most appropriate for you. You should not have a massage if you have an inflamed or infectious skin condition.

● WHAT HAPPENS AT A CONSULTATION

Sessions last up to an hour and a half (if you have a full body massage), and it is advisable not to eat a heavy meal before your appointment. The therapist will take a full case history including details of your lifestyle, general health and medical history plus any medication you may be taking. You'll be left to undress (you can keep your underwear on if you prefer) and will be asked to lie on a treatment couch. You will then be covered with a towel.

The treatment room may be softly lit and gentle background music may be playing to help you relax. If the therapist is using essential oils she may ask you if there are any particular oils that you like or she may just select the most appropriate blend.

The therapist will use different movements and techniques depending on your condition. The massage should be relaxing, although in tense areas of your body it may be painful. Always tell the therapist if an area hurts too much. At the end you'll be left alone for a few minutes to relax and gather your thoughts.

Treatment can have instant benefits but it usually requires a course of treatments to produce significant improvements. To start with, it will help to relieve pain and tension. Once the pain has subsided, the therapist will be able to work on the underlying cause of the problem.

Choosing a practitioner
Contact the British Massage Therapy Council,
17 Rymers Lane, Oxford OX4 3JU
Tel. 01865 774123   www.bmtc.co.uk

Meditation

For thousands of years meditation has been associated with religion, including Christianity, Judaism, Islam, Buddhism and Hinduism, and only recently has it been removed from its religious context, mainly due to the influence of the Maharishi Mahesh Yogi who together with the Beatles introduced Transcendental Meditation (TM) to the West.

The ancient yogis regarded meditation as a powerful tonic that boosted the body's energy and generated positive thoughts that could rejuvenate cells and slow down ageing. Now science is proving the yogis were right.

There are many different meditation techniques but all involve focusing your mind on an object or activity to which you can return if you become distracted. This

focus may be your breath, a mantra – a word or phrase that you repeat over and over through your meditation session – or a physical object such as a candle or fresh flowers.

The amount of time you spend meditating will differ depending on the method you learn, but just a few minutes a day can be effective in improving your quality of life.

Meditation can help you to deal with a particular problem or to achieve your goals. It acts on both the mind and the body so benefits affect all areas of your life, especially relationships. The physical benefits of meditation are many and include lower adrenaline levels, lower blood pressure, slower breathing and less stress on the cardiovascular system.

● CONDITIONS TREATED

Stress, anxiety, high blood pressure, headaches, fatigue, depression, insomnia, and chronic pain.

● WHO CAN'T BE TREATED?

Consult your doctor before starting meditation if you have a history of psychiatric problems.

● WHAT HAPPENS AT A CONSULTATION

While you can learn to meditate from books and tapes, consulting a teacher is a more effective way of getting started. Sessions may be individual or on a group basis. The space in which you are taught should be quiet and peaceful and you will be shown how to sit in a comfortable position. If you are learning TM your teacher will also give you a mantra to repeat in your head.

A session usually lasts between ten and 20 minutes, but some meditations can be as short as five minutes. Once you have learned the technique you will be encouraged to practise daily to benefit fully from it.

Choosing a practitioner
Contact the Transcendental Meditation Association, Freepost, London SW1P 4YY Tel. 0990 143733

Metamorphic Technique

Metamorphic Technique (MT) was developed in the 1960s by a British naturopath and reflexologist, Robert St John. Practitioners of MT believe that your feet represent your whole being from the time you were conceived, and that the physical, mental, and emotional patterns of your life are mapped out on the side of your foot and hand (which represents the spine). By working on these areas, therapists claim to be able to create an environment that allows change to take place. MT practitioners believe that each and every one of us has a life-force that always works for the good of the individual and that can change us into something better. Consequently, the practitioner's role is to act as a catalyst that sets your life-force in motion.

● CONDITIONS TREATED

MT is not a cure, rather it is a means of helping you to fulfil your potential and deal with long-term physical and mental illness, disability or handicap. It is also used to help hyperactive children or those with learning difficulties, Down's syndrome, or autism.

● WHO CAN'T BE TREATED?

MT can be used to treat people of all ages in any state of health, including pregnant women and women in labour.

● WHAT HAPPENS AT A CONSULTATION

Because it is important for the practitioner to remain detached from you, she won't take your case history or want any details about your life. Therapists believe that such information could be counterproductive. You'll be asked to remove your shoes and socks and sit comfortably while she works on each foot, using light circular movements. After about 20 minutes she will work on your hands and then finish the session by repeating the process on your head. The whole session takes about an hour. The practitioner may recommend that you go back in a week or wait to see if you want another treatment.

Choosing a practitioner
Contact the UK Metamorphic Association,
67 Ritherdon Road, Tooting, London SW17 8QE
Tel. 020 8672 5951

Moor therapy

See HYDROTHERAPY

Music therapy

Music therapy was developed in the 1940s as a means of helping war veterans to deal with stress and trauma. It proved so successful that musicians were soon being employed in hospitals to help those with all manner of mental illnesses and disturbances. Today music is often used in intensive care units and delivery rooms to help ease anxiety and pain.

Practitioners believe that the way you sing or communicate musically with others can provide an insight into your emotional problems. Music not only forms a link between people but it can also be used to symbolise feelings and can be an effective means of accessing emotions that people find too painful to verbalise.

● CONDITIONS TREATED

Learning difficulties, autism, hyperactivity in children, mental, emotional and behavioural problems, depression, stress, anxiety, pain relief, Alzheimer's disease.

● WHO CAN'T BE TREATED?

In the hands of a qualified therapist it can be used to help most people.

● WHAT HAPPENS AT A CONSULTATION

The therapy session may take place on a one-to-one basis or in a group. Adult sessions usually last an hour and children's about half an hour. Before treatment begins you will meet up with your therapist for an initial assessment. At this meeting she will want to discuss your problems and what you hope to gain from the treatment. She will also ask about your lifestyle and relationships, both now and in the past. This meeting is also a time for you to ask questions and air any concerns you have.

Treatment will normally start with the practitioner playing or singing a tune. You will be encouraged to sing or improvise on percussion instruments. The therapist will offer support and help you work through your feelings with the music.

Choosing a practitioner
Contact The Association of Professional Music Therapists, 26 Hamlyn Road, Glastonbury, Somerset BA6 8HT Tel. 01458 834919

Naturopathy

The system of naturopathy grew out of the 'nature cures' popular in 19th-century spa towns in Austria and Germany, which promoted the healing powers of fresh air, sunlight and exercise. Naturopaths believe that the human body has the power to heal itself, and that this power, known as the 'vital force', helps to maintain a healthy equilibrium known as homeostasis. However factors such as bad diet, injury, destructive emotions, lack of exercise and environmental pollutants can create an imbalance in this state of homeostasis, leading to illness.

The aim of the naturopath is to find the cause of the imbalance, help the vital force to eliminate it, and

to balance. Naturopaths also regard the symptoms of disease as a positive sign that the body is attempting to heal itself and believe that they should not be suppressed. An acute, short-lived illness such as flu is regarded as normal in a healthy body.

● CONDITIONS TREATED

Anaemia, allergies, arthritis, candida, circulation problems, constipation, cystitis, skin conditions such as eczema, premenstrual syndrome, sinusitis, ulcers, fatigue, high blood pressure.

● WHO CAN'T BE TREATED?

Naturopathy, when practised by a qualified practitioner, can be used to treat most people including young children, most elderly patients and pregnant women.

● **WHAT HAPPENS AT A CONSULTATION**

The initial appointment will last about an hour. The practitioner will want to build up a complete picture of your physical and emotional health. Standard medical checks are carried out plus naturopathic ones, which include examining the irises, analysing sweat or hair- and muscle-testing. As many naturopaths are trained as osteopaths, you may also be asked to undress so that the therapist can assess your body's structural alignment. He may also refer you for X-rays and blood tests.

The treatment itself will comprise recommendations for dietary changes and sometimes a cleansing fast, and, if necessary, hydrotherapy and osteopathy to build up your strength and immunity. Counselling, meditation or relaxation exercises may also be suggested.

Choosing a practitioner
Contact the General Council and Register of Naturopaths, Goswell House, 2 Goswell Road, Street, Somerset BA16 0JG Tel. 01458 840072

See also, AYURVEDA, FASTING

Nutritional therapy

Nutritional therapy is a relative newcomer to the world of alternative health. While it has its roots in NATUROPATHY, it was established as an holistic practice in its own right in the early 1980s. Nutritional therapists believe that vitamin and mineral deficiencies which are not significant enough to cause well-recognised diseases such as scurvy can still dramatically affect the way the body functions. Food, it is claimed, is at the root of all the chemical processes which occur in the body, so that all types of ill health can result from a lack of nutrients. Many are so common that you may not even identify the symptoms as a problem, for example fatigue, frequent coughs and colds, skin

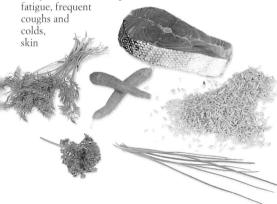

ailments and a whole host of niggling complaints which are all common symptoms of sub-clinical or minor nutrient deficiency. Practitioners use special diets and nutritional supplements to treat and prevent illness and restore the body to full health.

● CONDITIONS TREATED

Nutritional therapy can be used to combat almost all forms of ill health, but it is most commonly used to treat digestive disorders, migraine, premenstrual syndrome, fatigue, skin conditions such as acne and psoriasis, rheumatism and arthritis, high blood pressure, osteoporosis and multiple sclerosis.

● WHO CAN'T BE TREATED?

It can be used to treat anyone from babies and pregnant women to young children and the elderly. However there are a number of ailments for which it would be dangerous to take certain supplements, which is why it is always best to see a professionally qualified practitioner.

● WHAT HAPPENS AT A CONSULTATION

Your appointment will typically take about an hour, during which time the therapist will want to take your full case history, assessing your diet, lifestyle, and emotional wellbeing, as well as asking whether you take any medication or drugs. You may also be given a questionnaire to complete and some therapists may recommend hair, muscle, urine, sweat and muscle tests to pinpoint specific deficiencies. The practitioner will take into account any signs of food intolerance and toxic overload when forming an assessment. Based on all this information the therapist will then develop a diet plan for you that may include certain supplements. You may be asked to eliminate some foods from your diet for a number of weeks until the food allergy or intolerance is confirmed. Some practitioners also use herbal treatments and recommend exercise programmes. Follow-up sessions usually last 15 to 20 minutes.

Choosing a practitioner
Contact the Society for the Promotion of Nutritional Therapy at its website
www.nutrition–therapy.org
or the Institute for Optimum Nutrition, Blades Court, Deodar Road, London SW15 2NU Tel. 020 8877 9993

Osteopathy

Osteopathy was developed in 1874 by an American army doctor, Andrew Taylor Still. Horrified by the medical practices of the time, he rejected orthodox medicine and decided to seek out a new approach. He believed that the human body was a perfect piece of design and that illness was a direct result of strain placed on its structure. This strain could come from any number of sources including injury, poor posture, or negative emotions such as stress, anxiety and fear. He reasoned that manipulating the body's structure (the skeleton, muscles, ligaments, and connective tissue) to relieve the strain would enable the body to heal itself.

Cranial osteopathy involves manipulation of the head area and spine and many parents choose this therapy for treating young children.

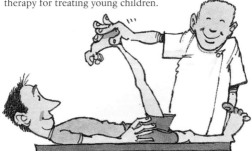

They are very different techniques, though. The osteopathy used to treat children is the same as that for adults but gentler techniques are applied to treat problem areas.

● CONDITIONS TREATED

Back and neck pain, arthritis and other joint pains, sciatica, sports and repetitive strain injuries, headache, insomnia, depression, menstrual pain, constipation, asthma and pregnancy conditions such as backache. It can also help children with colic, catarrh or glue ear.

● WHO CAN'T BE TREATED?

People with weak or fragile bone conditions, such as osteoporosis; people with inflamed joints from rheumatoid arthritis; and people with broken bones or bone cancer.

● WHAT HAPPENS AT A CONSULTATION

At your first appointment the practitioner will want to gather as much information about you as possible. She will ask about your symptoms, medical history, any old injuries, lifestyle, work and emotional health. If you have any pain, she will want to know what type of pain it is and how often you experience it.

She will also want to examine your body framework and posture, for which you will be asked to undress to your underwear. She will note how your spine curves and your muscle tone, and test your joints for ease of movement. Depending on your problem you may need further tests or X-rays. Standard medical tests will also be carried out.

You will then be asked to lie down on a treatment couch and the osteopath will usually begin with soft tissue massage to relax your muscles. This may be followed by more vigorous manipulation, including the painless high-velocity thrust that can cause the joint to make a disconcerting popping noise. Manipulation is not usually painful but you may feel stiff for a day or two after treatment and some people experience mild flu-like symptoms.

Your first consultation usually lasts for about an hour; follow-up sessions are shorter.

Choosing a practitioner
Contact the Osteopathic Information Service, General Osteopathic Council, 176 Tower Bridge Road, London SE1 3LU
020 7357 6655

Oxygen-ozone therapy

The practice of using oxygen to treat infection began over a century ago. In the UK it is still relatively unknown but in Germany alone there are more than 5,000 regulated practitioners. Therapists believe that the root cause of many diseases is a lack of oxygen. They believe that introducing a mixture of normal oxygen and its unstable form ozone into your blood improves its viscosity. Furthermore, the ozone's extra molecule of oxygen binds with anything that is not protected by an antioxidant: while healthy cells have built-in antioxidant protection, viruses, funguses and bacteria do not. Thus, weakened as they are by the ozone, they can then be handled by your body's natural defences.

● CONDITIONS TREATED

Heart and circulatory diseases, colonic disorders, certain cancers, auto-immune diseases, stroke, arthritis, multiple sclerosis, allergies, burns, and fungal, bacterial, and viral infections. It is also a controversial treatment for Aids.

● WHO CAN'T BE TREATED?

Oxygen-ozone therapy should be avoided by people who have recently had a heart attack or internal bleeding, people with hyperthyroidism, and those with a low blood platelet count.

● WHAT HAPPENS AT A CONSULTATION

Practitioners are medically qualified doctors. You will first be given a very thorough physical examination. Your practitioner will then explain what she has found and whether or not she feels that oxygen-ozone therapy is appropriate for you. If it is, treatment can be given daily or weekly.

The most common way that practitioners introduce ozone into the blood is by a process known as major autohemotherapy: a small quantity of blood is taken from you, then a mixture of oxygen-ozone is forced into it. As the ozone dissolves in your blood, oxygen atoms attack viruses and bacteria but do not harm healthy blood cells. This strengthened blood is then reintroduced intravenously to your body where it imparts some of its anti-bacterial and anti-viral properties to the rest of your blood as it is circulated. In addition to oxygen-ozone therapy your practitioner may also prescribe a programme of supplements.

Choosing a practitioner
Contact Derek Wolfe, Newton Mill, New St Petrock, nr Holsworthy EX22 7LP; send an sae for a list of practitioners. Or contact the Liongate Clinic, 8 Chilston Road, Tunbridge Wells, Kent TN4 Tel. 01892 543535

Polarity therapy

Polarity was developed in America by Dr Randolph Stone. Born in Austria in 1890, Stone's interest in healing led him to look beyond his conventional medical training to complementary health systems and therapies including naturopathy, osteopathy, herbalism, acupressure, chiropractic and reflexology. It took Stone 50 years to develop polarity therapy, which combines Eastern and Western approaches to health.

Stone based his system on the belief that a healthy body is one in which vital energy can flow freely

around it between two poles (positive and negative), with illness occurring as a result of a blockage in this flow. The polarity therapist's aim is to free these blockages to help the healing process and also to resolve the problems that caused the blockage in the first place.

● CONDITIONS TREATED

Allergies, back pain, digestive problems, ME (myalgic encephalitis), and respiratory, cardiovascular and digestive problems. It's also useful during pregnancy and for stress-related problems.

● WHO CAN'T BE TREATED?

It is suitable for most people provided it is practised by a qualified therapist.

● WHAT HAPPENS AT A CONSULTATION

At the first consultation the therapist will take a full medical history and will ask you about your home life, diet and exercise as well as your current health. This can take quite some time; if there is sufficient time left the therapist will start some bodywork; if not, treatment will begin on your second appointment.

For the bodywork you'll be asked to undress to your underwear (loose, thin clothing is acceptable if you prefer) and to lie on a treatment table. The therapist will work on specific points applying different degrees of pressure. The therapist will also provide emotional support to help you work through your problems, and will suggest dietary changes, if needed, and stretching yoga-like postures, the combined effects of which are designed to stimulate energy flow.

> **Choosing a practitioner**
> Contact the United Kingdom Polarity Therapy Association, Monomark House, 27 Old Gloucester Street, London WC1N 3XX
> Tel. 0700 705 2748

Psionic medicine
See RADIONICS

Psychodrama
See DRAMA THERAPY

Psychosynthesis
See PSYCHOTHERAPY & COUNSELLING

Psychotherapy and counselling

Psychotherapy and counselling are both general terms for a number of different talking treatments used to ease psychological suffering. Both originated in the work of Sigmund Freud, the father of psychoanalysis, and there is considerable controversy as to whether there is any real difference between the two disciplines.

The Royal College of Psychiatrists makes a distinction between 'lay' counsellors and consultant psychotherapists who are qualified in both medicine and psychiatry. But in the main counsellors and psychotherapists have a lot in common, the main difference being that counselling tends to be called on for specific problems, in times when you find it hard to cope, while psychotherapy tends to involve more intensive longer-lasting treatment. Here's a round-up of the main approaches used to enable you to find a talking therapy that's best for you.

Counselling – this allows you to talk over specific problems such as bereavement or divorce. A counsellor will prompt you to talk freely, will dig less deeply than a psychotherapist and proffer little or no advice. Instead she will aim to reflect your thoughts and feelings back to you in a way that encourages self-awareness and enables you to view situations from different perspectives.

Psychodynamic approach – this is an umbrella term for psychoanalysis, psychotherapy and analytical psychology. The common link is the importance placed on the subconscious mind. The practitioner works to discover how childhood experiences influence your present problems by exploring your dreams, fantasies, fears and desires. Treatment tends to be long-term, the most intensive being psychoanalysis, involving five sessions a week over a number of years.

Humanistic approach – this form of therapy encourages you to reach your full potential and to reach a better understanding of yourself. It aims to help people to explore their feelings and take responsibility for their own thoughts and actions. Practitioners focus on self-development rather than neuroses.

Humanistic therapies include:
– GESTALT THERAPY.

– *Psychosynthesis* (sometimes called the 'psychology of the soul') in which practitioners use painting, movement, and writing to enable you to recognise and value different parts of your personality.

– *Transactional analysis,* based on the idea that you have a parent, adult and child within your personality which helps you to understand your responses to other people.

– *Transpersonal therapy*, in which practitioners use stories and ritual to enable people to transcend themselves and feel in touch with the universe.

– *Psychodrama*, in which you are encouraged to act out your personal dramas in a group situation.

– *Primal therapy*, which takes you back to relive the trauma of birth and infancy in a cathartic way.

– *Re-birthing*, which uses breathing techniques to re-experience the trauma of birth and release tension which leads to fears in adult life.

Behavioural/cognitive therapies – these are based on the notion that you need not find the cause of your problems in order to solve them, but that you can simply learn new ways of thinking and behaving. Cognitive and behavioural therapists also teach stress-management techniques.

The therapies include:

– *Behavioural therapy*: Practitioners believe that behaviour is learnt in relation to past experiences and so can be unlearnt without looking at why the pattern formed in the first place.

– *Cognitive therapy*: Practitioners believe in the power of the mind to affect behaviour. By learning to spot, question, and change negative or self-destructive emotions, you can change habitual responses and behaviour.

– *Cognitive analytical therapy*: Practitioners assist you to find ways of drawing on your inner resources to change negative patterns of thinking and behaving.

– *Cognitive behavioural therapy*: Practitioners combine cognitive and behavioural techniques so treatment may involve relaxation techniques and strategies to help you change your thoughts.

– *Neurolinguistic programming*: This is a blend of cognitive behavioural techniques and humanistic psychotherapy. Practitioners claim that life experiences from birth onwards programme the way in which you see the world. A therapist will help you to take control of your actions and change the way you talk and your body language.

– *Personal construct therapy*: Therapists aim to unlock your view of the world using questionnaires and role play.

– *Brief therapy*: This consists of four one-hour sessions. In the first the practitioner aims to work out the cause of your problem and the next two focus on techniques to deal with it. There is a three-month gap then a follow-up session to assess progress. It is useful for dealing with stress.

– *The 12-step programme*: This is taught in weekly group sessions over several years. The first step is to acknowledge your problem and the last step includes a promise to help others in the same situation.

● CONDITIONS TREATED

Stress, anxiety, panic attacks, depression, phobias, eating disorders, grief, relationship problems, sexual problems, psychosomatic illness and personal development.

● WHO CAN'T BE TREATED?

Avoid psychoanalysis, psychotherapy or counselling if you have a psychotic illness such as schizophrenia or manic depression.

Choosing a practitioner
Contact the British Association for Counselling, 1 Regent Place, Rugby, Warwickshire CV21 2PJ Tel. 01788 578328; the UK Council for Psychotherapy, 167-169 Great Portland Street, London WC1 5FB Tel. 020 7436 3002; or the British Confederation of Psychotherapists, 37a Mapesbury Road, London, NW2 4HJ Tel. 020 8830 5173

● WHAT HAPPENS AT A CONSULTATION

Your first appointment is a good chance to see if you feel at ease with the type of therapy you have chosen. The practitioner will want to know what kind of help you're looking for and will decide whether she can help you. Sometimes this first appointment is offered free of charge, especially if treatment is likely to be long-term. You may find that distressing emotions are released in the course of a treatment and a trained practitioner will be able to help you through these. Sessions usually last about an hour and are held once a week. The length of treatment depends on the approach and can last from a few months to several years.

Qigong

Qigong (also known as chi kung, and pronounced *chee gong*) means 'energy work'. It is not a martial art but a holistic system that combines breathing techniques with precise movements and mental concentration. Its movements are designed to unblock stagnant energy so as to allow it to flow freely around your body and boost health and wellbeing.

● CONDITIONS TREATED

Fatigue, stress-related conditions, high blood pressure, heart disease, musculo-skeletal pain.

● WHO CAN'T BE TREATED?

It is suitable for people of all ages and levels of fitness including young children and the elderly.

● WHAT HAPPENS AT A CONSULTATION

Qigong is usually taught in groups but you can get one-to-one lessons if you prefer. Lessons don't require any special equipment. Loose, comfortable clothing should be worn, and flat flexible shoes rather than trainers. You will be taught a series of exercises and correct breathing essential to qigong. The exercises can be performed in any order.

You will start by repeating each one six times and it's left to you to build up the number of sets when you feel ready. Lessons run for about an hour and end with an exercise designed to still your mind and body. Ideally, qigong should be practised every day if only for five or ten minutes each time.

Choosing a practitioner
Contact the Tse Qigong Centre, PO Box 116,
Manchester M20 3YN Tel: 0161 929 4485

Radionics

Developed in the 1920s by American neurologist Albert Abramas, radionics is a method of health analysis and treatment. Practitioners believe that by working in the energy field that surrounds each and every one of us, they can improve the body's own self-healing ability.

Radionics is a form of absent healing, meaning you may never see your practitioner in person. Using what they call a witness – usually a lock of your hair – practitioners are able to read your energy levels because your hair is still linked to its energy source, no matter how far apart you and your practitioner are. Treatment is also administered at a distance. Your practitioner will send energy via the witness to alter your body's own energy field and to enable it to destroy the disease.

Abramas' work was opposed by the US medical establishment and it is illegal to practise radionics there. However, a UK medical committee set up in the 1920s found his methods surprisingly accurate.

Similar to radionics is a system of healing called psionic medicine. Practitioners claim that it works by detecting and rebalancing disruptions in a person's bio-energy. Therapists dowse patients to diagnose their condition and use homeopathic remedies to treat them.

● CONDITIONS TREATED

Hay fever, asthma, and arthritis can all be relieved, but the main aim of radionics is to improve overall health.

● WHO CAN'T BE TREATED?

It is extremely safe for people of all ages and can even be used on animals. However, for very young children or the very sick it is advisable to ensure that their doctor is informed.

● WHAT HAPPENS AT A CONSULTATION

In most cases, you won't see a practitioner in person. Instead you'll be sent a questionnaire asking about your medical history, current health problems and any medication you may be taking, lifestyle, interests, and personality. The form is then sent back to the therapist. You may also be asked to include a lock of hair ('witness'). The practitioner will use the information in the questionnaire, together with your hair, to tune into your vibration and assess your body structure, emotional state, energy level and your tendency to particular conditions. The therapist will then write to you explaining what she has found and how she means to treat you.

Radionics practitioners use a sophisticated piece of equipment called an automatic computerised treatment system (ACTS) which contains thousands of treatments including homeopathy, herbalism, sound and light therapy. The ACTS is linked to you via your witness and delivers the appropriate treatment for your needs just when you need it and in the right quantity. If necessary you may also be advised to see your doctor or other health professional such as a homeopath.

Choosing a practitioner
The Confederation of Radionic and Radiesthesic Organisations, c/o The Maperton Trust, Wincanton, Somerset BA9 8EH
Tel. 01963 32651

Reflexology

The exact origins of reflexology are unknown, but the Chinese are thought to have practised a form of it as many as 5,000 years ago. It wasn't until the early 20th century, however, that reflexology began to take shape in the West. In 1913 an American consultant, Dr William Fitzgerald, developed a system of healing called zone  therapy. He found that he could divide the body into ten vertical zones, from the tips of the toes to the top of the head and back down to the fingertips, and that there was an energy link between parts of the body found on the same zone. By applying pressure to the appropriate parts of the hands, which he did by clipping clothes pegs to the fingertips, he was able to reduce pain in other parts of the body. Fitzgerald's methods were later refined and renamed reflexology by another American, Eunice Ingham. She discovered that by applying pressure to certain areas of the feet, she not only relieved pain but could treat a range of other ailments, too.

Reflexologists believe that work on small parts of the body can be used to treat the whole body. They believe that the feet (and hands) mirror the rest of the body, so that if you lie with your feet together their shape not only matches that of your body but your organs and body parts would appear on your feet in the same position that they do in your body. These are called reflex points. Therapists believe that by applying pressure to these reflex points they can stimulate or rebalance energy in the related zone and trigger the body's own healing system.

● CONDITIONS TREATED

Digestive and menstrual problems, stress, fatigue, general aches and pains, eczema, glue ear.

● WHO CAN'T BE TREATED?

It is suitable for everyone from children to the elderly provided you are treated by a qualified practitioner. Tell your therapist if you are in the early stages of pregnancy so that she can tailor the treatment accordingly.

• WHAT HAPPENS AT A CONSULTATION

The therapist starts the session by asking questions about you, your medical history, work, diet and lifestyle. She will also want to know if you are currently seeing a doctor or taking any medication.

For your treatment you'll be asked to sit in a reclining chair or lie on a treatment couch The therapist may wipe your feet with witch hazel-soaked cotton wool and apply talcum powder or lotion to your feet to make it easier to carry out the treatment.

The therapist will work over the whole of your foot, before attending to specific areas. Several techniques are used to work your foot, but more often than not therapists use their thumb or index finger. If you experience any pain or tenderness it's a sign of blocked energy in the corresponding part of your body. To free the blockage and stimulate healing your therapist will spend time working on any problem areas she finds.

The first appointment usually lasts about an hour and a half to allow for the consult-ation; subsequent appointments will take half an hour to an hour.

Choosing a practitioner
Contact the Association of Reflexologists, 27 Old Gloucester Street, London WC1N 3XX Tel. 0990 673320

Reiki

Reiki is the Japanese word for 'universal life-force'. As with Traditional Chinese Medicine, it is based on the idea that the life-force is what animates you and flows in and around your body along meridians or pathways, and a blockage in this flow will cause illness.

Reiki was developed at the end of the 19th century by a Japanese Christian theologian, Mikao Usui. He was so challenged by the healing powers of Christ as told in the Bible that he dedicated his life to searching for the answer. Years of study and meditation culminated in Reiki, a system of healing in which the practitioner makes himself into a channel for energy to flow into

the patient where it is received at the point(s) of greatest need or imbalance to assist healing.

● CONDITIONS TREATED

Reiki is received and used by the patient in the way it is needed. This means that it can help with all forms of illness whether it be an acute physical problem or a long-term emotional one.

● WHO CAN'T BE TREATED?

Reiki is suitable for everyone even children, pregnant women and people in the stages of terminal illness.

● WHAT HAPPENS AT A CONSULTATION

For a treatment you'll be asked to lie down fully clothed on a couch and relax. The practitioner gently places his hands for a few minutes at a time in a sequence of positions covering the whole body. Each session lasts about an hour.

Choosing a practitioner
Contact the Reiki Association, Cornbrook Bridge House, Clee Hill, Ludlow, Shropshire SY8 3QQ Tel. 01981 550829

Relaxation

See BREATHING AND RELAXATION

Rolfing

Rolfing was developed by American biochemist Dr Ida P. Rolf in the 1930s. It is based on her belief that gravity, injuries and bad postural habits picked up from, say, sitting at uncomfortable school desks affect your body's alignment and lead to structural imbalances which, in turn, affect the body as a whole.

She found that by manipulating the connective tissue that surrounds and links all the muscles she could reshape a body that has been pulled out of alignment. The aim is to realign the body's structure and restore balance, so that the body can heal itself. Practitioners also teach you how to move so that you move with gravity rather than against it.

Sometimes treatment can bring deeply buried emotional issues to the surface, and a well-trained therapist will know how to deal with this if it happens.

● CONDITIONS TREATED

Most conditions related to bad posture respond well to Rolfing. These include back pain, neck, shoulder and joint pain, asthma and digestive problems.

● WHO CAN'T BE TREATED?

Rolfing is suitable for both adults and children, but should be avoided by anyone with an inflammatory disease such as rheumatoid arthritis or cancer.

Choosing a practitioner
Contact Rolfing UK, PO Box 14793,
London SW1V 2WB
Tel. 0117 946 6374

● WHAT HAPPENS AT A CONSULTATION

A course of Rolfing usually comprises ten sessions, each lasting between an hour and an hour and a half. In the first session the practitioner will take details of your medical history. For the treatment you will be asked to strip down to your underwear, but this is not obligatory. Some (but not all) Rolfers will take your photograph throughout the course. In each session the practitioner works on a different part of your body. The first usually focuses on realigning the rib cage to 'free the breath'. Rolfers use their hands, fingertips, knuckles and even their elbows to manipulate the connective tissue. You may have moments of discomfort during the treatment, but these are quickly followed by a deep sense of relief.

Schüssler salts

See BIOCHEMIC TISSUE SALTS

Sensory integration therapy

See SOUND THERAPY

Shamanism

See HEALING

Shiatsu

Shiatsu is a therapy that works on the mind, body and spirit. Historically it developed from two healing systems: Traditional Chinese Medicine and ancient methods of folk massage in the Far East. But it eventually became more firmly established in Japan. In Shiatsu illness is seen in terms of the classical Chinese model: resulting from an imbalance of your vital energy (*chi*). The aim of treatment is to balance the flow of energy around the body's 12 meridians.

Shiatsu is the Japanese word for 'finger pressure'. However, as well as their fingers practitioners also use their palms, elbows, arms, knees and feet to apply

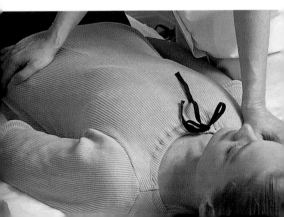

pressure to the same acupoints (*tsubos*) as those used
in acupressure and acupuncture to free up the
meridians and restore a harmonious energy flow.

● CONDITIONS TREATED

Back pain, migraine, anxiety, rheumatism, asthma,
insomnia, impotence, painful periods, fatigue and
depression can all be treated. Shiatsu also improves
general health by stimulating the circulation and
immune system, balancing hormones and relieving
stress.

● WHO CAN'T BE TREATED?

Anyone with blood or lymphatic cancer should not
undergo shiatsu treatment. Otherwise treatment
from a professional practitioner is safe for anyone,
even small children, pregnant women and the
elderly.

● WHAT HAPPENS AT A CONSULTATION

Practitioners diagnose according to the four classic
Oriental methods: asking, observation, listening
and touching. So in addition to giving your case
history, you may also be asked to show your
tongue.

The therapist will ask you to lie down and will use
palpation (diagnostic touch) on your back and
abdomen, checking for signs of energy imbalance.

Some therapists also take readings from the pulse points on the wrists that acupuncturists use. You should take with you details of any medication that you are taking.

Treatment usually takes place on a mat. The therapist will use pressure and stretches to stimulate or soothe the length of the meridians as well as focusing on specific points. You will be fully dressed during the treatment so it is a good idea to wear loose, comfortable clothing.

An appointment usually lasts about an hour with most of the time being taken up by the treatment. Short-term 'healing reactions' such as a headache or flu-like symptoms for 24 hours are not unusual after treatment. These are positive signs that toxins and emotions are being released. The number of follow-up sessions required will depend on the condition being treated.

Choosing a practitioner
Contact the Shiatsu Society of the UK, Eastlands Court, St Peter's Road, Rugby, Warwickshire CV21 3QP
Tel. 01788 555051

Sound therapy

In the ancient Greek, Egyptian, and Indian civilisations the power of sound and vibration was held to be the basic creative force of the universe. But it wasn't until the late 19th century that doctors recognised the therapeutic benefits of sound. Sound therapists believe that every organ in your body vibrates at a healthy resonant frequency and that disease is simply a part of your body vibrating out of time. By working with the voice or electronic or musical instruments, sound

therapists claim to be able to restore balance in the body and encourage self-healing.

The Greek mathematician Pythagoras developed a theory known as 'the music of the spheres', which held that the planets create harmonically linked sounds as they move through the universe, and he taught his students about the secrets of healing with sound.

● CONDITIONS TREATED

Stress, anxiety, high blood pressure, migraine, depression, autism, dyslexia, pain relief, muscle and joint pain.

● WHO CAN'T BE TREATED?

Sound therapy is suitable for people of all ages and levels of fitness, including children.

● WHAT HAPPENS AT A CONSULTATION

Depending on the method, sessions may be on a one-to-one or group basis. Treatment usually lasts an hour and is given weekly over a number of months. Chanting tends to be taught in weekend workshops. There are a number of approaches:

Chanting – you are taught how to use your voice to create pure sound. The aim is not to sing perfectly but to make sounds with a healing vibration.

Tomatis method – devised by Dr Alfred Tomatis, a French ear, nose and throat specialist. The treatment consists of a programme of filtered music, especially Mozart and Gregorian chants, played through headphones to encourage the ear to listen properly. Although Tomatis' theories are controversial, the results have been so successful that it is used by musicians and singers, psychologists, and speech, music and occupational therapists, to treat both adults and children.

Choosing a practitioner
Contact the Tomatis Centre UK Ltd, 3 Wallands
Crescent, Lewes, East Sussex BN7 2QT
Tel. 01273 474877; The Hale Clinic, 7 Park Crescent,
London N3 2NL Tel. 020 7631 0156, for details of
AIT; Chris James at Sounds Wonderful, PO Box
2541, Bath BA3 6XY Tel. 08700 768637; or write to
The Natural Voice Practitioners Network, Droridge
Barn, Dartington, Devon TQ9 6JG

Auditory Integration Therapy (AIT) – developed
by Dr Guy Berard, a disciple of Tomatis. Like the
Tomatis method, treatment consists of playing a
programme of music through headphones to
encourage the ear to listen properly, but all types of
music can be played.

Cymatic – developed by UK osteopath Dr Peter
Manners, but his therapy is practised most
commonly in the US. Practitioners use a machine
that transmits sound waves through the skin to a
specific area of your body, to encourage the cells to
vibrate at a healthy optimum resonance.

Spiritual healing

See HEALING (SPIRITUAL)

T'ai chi

The full name for t'ai chi is t'ai chi chuan. It is thought to have been founded between 960 and 1279 by a Taoist monk and martial arts expert Chang San Feng. A combination of non-combatative martial arts and meditation, t'ai chi is used to promote longevity and spiritual awareness.

There is a variety of different styles of t'ai chi, but common to all of them is the practice of the form – a set of defence movements performed in a specific pattern. They are practised slowly and gracefully to rebalance the flow of energy through the body along channels called meridians. This in turn encourages relaxation and harmonises the mind, body and spirit.

A form can be short or long. A short form typically comprises around 48 movements and takes about five to ten minutes to perform. A long form involves around 108 movements and can take up to an hour to perform.

● CONDITIONS TREATED

It can help stress-related conditions such as anxiety and high blood pressure. It can also help arthritis, recovery from injury and it can aid in rehabilitation following a heart attack.

● WHO CAN'T PRACTISE IT?

T'ai chi can be practised by people of all ages and levels of fitness.

● WHAT TO EXPECT IN A CLASS

T'ai chi is taught by a t'ai chi master. When choosing a class it's important that you feel happy with your teacher's qualifications. Classes take between 15 and 30 people and last for about an hour and a half. Individual lessons are also an option.

Wear loose, comfortable clothing with socks or flat shoes. As with any exercise class be sure to let the instructor know if you have any injuries or health problems that may make it difficult for you to perform certain movements.

The class will usually start with warm-up exercises after which you will be taught the components of a form. People are often surprised to learn that it can take up to a year to master a short form and as long as two years for a long one.

You should not feel sore and tired after a class and you'll be advised not to push yourself too hard, but mastering the movements does require continuous practice so you'll be advised to work on them at home, too.

Choosing a practitioner
Contact the UK T'ai Chi Association,
PO Box 159, Bromley, Kent BR1 3XX
Tel. 020 8289 5166

Temperature biofeedback training
See BIOFEEDBACK

Thalassotherapy
See HYDROTHERAPY

Therapeutic touch

Therapeutic touch (TT) is a form of healing developed in the 1970s by Dolores Krieger, a professor of nursing at New York University. She believed that we are all surrounded by an energy field in which illness or imbalances manifest themselves. This energy, she claimed, can be sent from one person to another and through the exchange healing takes place.

TT is based on nursing theory rather than spiritual or religious beliefs. It is seen as something that everybody can do and the practitioner is not seen as carrying out the healing itself, but facilitating a process that takes place in all of us. To be truly effective TT must be given by a genuine caring individual with the purest intentions to someone who is willing to receive it.

An insincere or inappropriate touch can, in fact, do more harm than good.

● CONDITIONS TREATED

It can help to relieve anxiety, reduce pain and speed up wound-healing. It also induces deep relaxation and offers comfort to terminally ill patients.

● WHO CAN'T BE TREATED?

It can be used for almost anyone, including the old, the dying, and the mentally ill, and in almost any situation including intensive care units and neonatal wards.

● WHAT HAPPENS AT A CONSULTATION

TT is practised mainly by nurses in hospitals and clinics. It is carried out in a series of steps, the main ones being as follows:

Centring – the practitioner becomes calm and focused so that the patient is able to get the full benefits of the treatment.

Assessment – the patient's energy is examined. The therapist holds her hands three to five inches away from the patient's body to scan their energy field and pick up any clues about the nature of the imbalance.

Clearing – the practitioner sweeps her hands the length of the patient's body without touching it to clear any problem areas picked up in the assessment.

Treatment – the practitioner aims to rebalance the patient's energy levels.

Evaluation – this takes place when the rebalancing feels complete.

Sessions generally last for about 30 minutes, although shorter treatments are given to babies, pregnant women, the frail, and the mentally ill.

Choosing a practitioner
For details of nurses trained in TT, contact the British Association of Therapeutic Touch, Redmire Farm, Mongrisdale, Penrith, Cumbria CA11 0TB
www.landhouse.co.uk/healing.asp

Traditional Chinese Medicine (TCM)

See ACUPUNCTURE, CHINESE HERBALISM, REIKI, SHIATSU, TUINA

Trager® Approach

Trager® was developed in Hawaii in the 1930s by Dr Milton Trager. It is based on the belief that the body is meant to be supple and flexible like a child's, but that as you get older your posture becomes distorted through, for example, sitting badly at desks, wearing high heels and suppressing emotions. This, according to Trager, interrupts the natural flow of energy round the body causing blockages and ultimately pain and ill health. Using gentle, rhythmic stretching movements, Trager® practitioners aim to re-educate their patients to use the body in a balanced way.

● CONDITIONS TREATED

Shoulder, back and knee pain; injuries (such as whiplash). It also promotes relaxation.

● WHO CAN'T BE TREATED?

This gentle therapy can be used to treat most people. Inform your practitioner if you have osteoporosis or thrombosis.

Choosing a practitioner
Contact The Trager Association UK,
40 Summerdale Road, Hove BN3 8LG
Tel. 01273 411193

● WHAT HAPPENS AT A CONSULTATION

A session lasts for about one and a half hours. At the first visit the therapist will take down details of your medical history. You will then be asked to undress to your underwear, but light clothing is acceptable if you feel more comfortable.

The therapist will work around your body gently rocking, rolling, stretching and pulling it to loosen joints and relax muscles. As the tension is released the healing process begins.

Transactional analysis

See PSYCHOTHERAPY

Tuina

Tuina (pronounced *tweena*) means push and grasp. It is part of the system of Traditional Chinese Medicine (TCM) and, like acupuncturists, practitioners of this therapy work on the meridians (invisible energy channels in the body) using their fingers to manipulate specific parts of the body, with rubbing, kneading and rolling actions to restore balance and recharge the body's energy levels.

● CONDITIONS TREATED

Stress-related and emotional conditions, neck pain, frozen shoulder, and back pain. Regular massage is said to be able to prevent illness.

● WHO CAN'T BE TREATED

Those with cancer and certain infections should not be treated. Inform the therapist if you have an infection of any kind.

● WHAT HAPPENS AT A CONSULTATION

Each session lasts about an hour, and at the initial visit the practitioner will want to build a picture of your medical history. The massage is very vigorous and the therapist will work on your muscles, spine and joints. She also works on specific pressure points that relate to certain organs, relieving pain and encouraging a healing response. Because each organ has an associated emotional response, tuina massage can also be emotionally cathartic.

Choosing a practitioner
Contact the BodyHarmonics Centre,
54 Flecker's Drive, Hatherly, Cheltenham GL51 5BD
Tel. 01242 582168

Visualisation

Visualisation is a technique that harnesses the power of the imagination in helping you to cope with stress, fulfil your potential, and trigger your body's own healing mechanism. It's been used by psychologists around the world since the mid-20th century to boost motivation and change negative habits and attitudes.

● CONDITIONS TREATED

Stress management, pain control, allergies, heart problems, anxiety, phobias, cancer, auto-immune diseases.

● WHO CAN'T BE TREATED?

It can be used to treat anyone including small children. But if you have a medical condition, visualisation should be done under the supervision of a practitioner; for example, patients who are mentally ill or experience hallucinations need to

consult a therapist trained in mental health. And
visualisations involving grass can trigger attacks in
people with allergies.

● WHAT HAPPENS AT A CONSULTATION

Visualisation can be practised on either an
individual or a group basis. The therapist will
probably begin by asking for details of your
medical history. She will also want to know what
you hope to gain from the therapy as this will
influence the choice of images you use.

Your treatment will start with a simple relaxation
exercise. Once you are relaxed and sitting or lying
down comfortably your therapist will guide you
through a visualisation. You will be encouraged to
picture your chosen images as vividly as possible.
You may also be asked to repeat affirmations such
as 'I am in control', to help replace negative
thoughts with positive ones.

The average session lasts between half an hour and
an hour, but the length is generally determined by
your needs. You will also be advised to practise the
technique at home on a daily basis.

Choosing a practitioner
Contact the United Kingdom Council for
Psychotherapy, 167-169 Great Portland Street,
London W1N 5FB Tel. 020 7436 3002

Yoga

Yoga was developed as a Hindu religious discipline to help rebalance the mental, physical and spiritual aspects of an individual's life. In the East yoga is practised as a means of working towards higher spiritual goals. For many people yoga is a wonderful way to relax and get fit, but its benefits go much further, helping to boost overall health and wellbeing.

● CONDITIONS TREATED

A daily yoga routine will help stress-related conditions such as headaches, high blood pressure, backache, insomnia and weight problems. Sufferers of arthritis, ME (myalgic encephalitis), premenstrual syndrome and menopausal problems can also benefit.

● WHO CAN'T PRACTISE IT?

Yoga can safely be practised by almost everyone from young children to the elderly, and even those who are unfit or overweight.

Choosing a class
Contact The British Wheel of Yoga,
1 Hamilton Place, Boston Road, Sleaford,
Lincolnshire NG34 7ES Tel. 01529 306851

● WHAT TO EXPECT IN A BEGINNERS' CLASS

A typical class will start with a relaxation exercise. This is followed by a sequence of asanas (yoga postures), that work every part of the body. As you perform each asana you will also be taught correct breathing and stretching techniques.

As a newcomer you will not be expected to try advanced postures. But with regular practice, you'll be surprised at how quickly your body becomes more supple. Each session will close with a period of deep relaxation designed to leave you feeling energised.

Zero balancing

Zero balancing, a combination of Western and Eastern medicines, was developed in the 1970s by an American doctor, osteopath and acupuncturist called Fritz Smith. It got its name after a client of Smith's described the treatment as having brought them back to their core balance.

Therapists believe that the body has an energy field which is related to the musculo-skeletal system. Practitioners use touch to encourage your body to adjust to its ideal shape and promote a smooth, steady energy flow, which will boost your body's self-healing abilities.

● **CONDITIONS TREATED**

Stress, headaches, migraine, structural problems
such as backache and shoulder pain, and improving
posture.

● **WHO CAN'T BE TREATED?**

People with hip and knee replacements, epilepsy,
ME (myalgic encephalitis) or a history of cancer.

● **WHAT HAPPENS AT A CONSULTATION**

Your session will probably begin with general
questions about whether you have a condition that
needs particular attention and whether you have
any pain or stress. But apart from that practitioners
don't require a huge amount of detail about your
medical history.

The treatment is performed fully clothed and you'll
be asked to lie on a treatment couch. Using a firm
but comfortable touch the practitioner will work
from your lower back down your legs and into your
feet then up the upper back and neck. A session
takes between twenty and forty minutes.

Choosing a practitioner
Contact the Zero Balancing Association UK,
10 Victoria Grove, Bridport, Dorset DT6 3AA
Tel. 01223 315480 e-mail: zbauk@aol.com

COLLINS GEM
1950s
a mine of information

COLLINS GEM
1960s
a mine of information

COLLINS GEM
1970s
NO GAS
a mine of information

COLLINS GEM
1980s
a mine of information

COLLINS   Jane's
CIVIL
AIRCRAFT
a mine of information

COLLINS GEM
CLANS
& Tartans
a mine of information

COLLINS GEM
Classic
TV SERIES
a mine of information

COLLINS   Jane's
COMBAT
AIRCRAFT
a mine of information

COLLINS GEM
FIRSTS
a mine of information

COLLINS GEM
GOLF
a mine of information

COLLINS GEM
HILLWALKER'S
Survival Guide
a mine of information

COLLINS GEM
HOME
EMERGENCY GUIDE
a mine of information

COLLINS GEM
Collecting
STAMPS
a mine of information

COLLINS GEM
STARS
a mine of information

COLLINS GEM
SUPERSTITIONS
a mine of information

COLLINS GEM
Using Your
SOFTWARE
a mine of information